D0113537

pocketbooks

Frontispiece: Noit Intercourse
John Latham, 1960 (courtesy of Lisson Gallery)

The Libraries of
Thought & Imagination

an anthology of books and bookshelves

The Libraries of
Thought & Imagination

Edited by Alec Finlay

pocketbooks
Morning Star Publications
Polygon

2001

Z
116
.A2
L 53
2001

Published by:
pocketbooks
Canongate Venture (5), New Street, Edinburgh, EH8 8BH.

Morning Star Publications
Canongate Venture (5), New Street, Edinburgh, EH8 8BH.

Polygon
22 George Square, Edinburgh, EH8 9LF.

Typeset in Minion and Univers.
Typesetting and artworking by Cluny Sheeler.
Design concept by Lucy Richards with Alec Finlay.
Printed and bound by Scotprint, Haddington.

Published with the assistance of grants from the Scottish Arts Council National
Lottery Fund, Scotland's Year of the Artist, and the Highlands and Islands Enterprise
(HI Arts),

ISBN 0 7486 6300 2

List of Contents

Editor's Acknowledgements

This anthology was edited during a residency funded by Scotland's Year of the Artist (SYOTA), hosted by the National Library of Scotland (NLS), May 2000–June 2001. In editing a book of books and bookshelves it is fitting that the greater part of the acknowledgements should be to librarians. At NLS I would like to thank Ann Matheson, the initial respondent, Murray Simpson, Robin Smith, and the Department of Special Collections, who hosted the residency, and Alan Marchbank, whose criticisms of the concept of an artist-initiated residency prompted me to refine the project at an early stage.

The residency was extended to a number of other libraries in the UK and USA each of which distributed a set of free bookmarks and supported this publication. I would like to thank the Scottish Poetry Library, Glasgow School of Art Library, Manchester Metropolitan University Library, National Art Library, Edinburgh College of Art Library, Edinburgh City Libraries & Central Library, Glasgow City Libraries & The Mitchell Library, East Lothian Library Services, Duncan of Jordanstone College of Art Library, University of Dundee Library, Robert Gordon University Library, Byam Shaw College of Art Library, the British Library, Lovejoy Library (Southern Illinois University), Amherst College Library, Holman Library (McKendree College), Sion Hill Library (Bath Spa University College). Other participants included Wigtown Book Festival, Printed Matter Bookstore, Woodland Pattern Book Centre and Hull Key Arts.

I would also like to thank Bill Allen, Simon Cutts, Hil Williamson, Jenny Renton (*Scottish Book Collector Magazine*), Catherine MacInerney, Ken Cockburn, Robyn Marsack, Sophy Dale, Jim Fiddes, Louisa Coles, Sune Nordgren, Kees Van Gelder, Amanda Keeley, Thomas Evans, Helen Douglas, Telfer Stokes and Richard Price.

I would like to thank Ken Cockburn, Alison Humphry, Vicky Hale, Sophy Dale, Laura Coxson, and Cluny Sheeler at pocketbooks; Lucy Richards; Alison Bowden and Emma Darling at Polygon; the staff at Scotprint. .

I would also like to thank Olaf Nicolai, who conceived the 'Imaginary Books' project. The selection that appears here is an extract from his ongoing project, 'Library of books that could exist'. Anyone who wishes to contribute to this should send their imaginary book (title, author, publisher and if required a brief description) to Olaf: nico@snafu.de. or to pocketbooks: info@pbks.co.uk. Selected contributions will form the basis of a catalogue of imagined books.

The title of the anthology, *The Libraries of Thought and Imagination*, is after a phrase of Emerson's: 'the libraries of thought and publication'; the title of the Foreword is taken from William Carlos Williams poem, 'Asphodel: that Greeny Flower'.

Dedicated to the memory of Hans Waanders (1951–2001)

Library – Always have one at home, particularly if you live in the country.

Gustav Flaubert, *Dictionary of Accepted Ideas,*
translated by Jacques Barzun.

'And so books entered our lives ...'

Books radiate imagination. Marked and creased, buckled by the heat of the sun, fluted by damp, they gather associations and furnish our intimate lives. Bookshelves: an array of ordered spines, muted colours, sheer and stratified, fusty with neglect, darkening a room; they bear down, greedy for attention.

The corpus of culture and its corpse, books carry our dreams and bear the deadweight of convention. Rational thought, ordered communication and liminal imagination are entangled in the book's paradoxical properties as the formality of the library threatens to smother the flames and generosities of the imagination. And yet the library is filled with tales of Romantic adventure. In *Les Mots* Sartre describes his excited discovery of his father's library:

> I never ... searched for nests ... never looked for plants or threw stones at birds. But books were my birds and nests, my pets, my stable and my countryside; the library was the world trapped in a mirror; it had its infinite breadth, its variety and unpredictability ... The *Grand Larousse* took the place of everything: I would pick a volume at random, from behind the desk, on the last-but-one shelf, A–Bello, Bello–Ch or Ci–D, Mele–Po or Pr–Z (these associations of proper syllables had become proper names indicating areas of human knowledge: there was the Ci–D region and Pr–Z region, with their fauna and flora, their towns, their great men and their battles) ... I met the universe in books: assimilated, classified, labelled and studied, but still impressive; and I confused the chaos of my experiences through books with the hazardous course of real events.

Sartre's memoir is an act of self-accusation for although the marvellous mirror-world of books was an escape from his cloistered childhood, his immersion in words was in retrospect, another form of confinement.

The book is a precise technology, with an intrinsic propriety, a formal logic that requires only to be unfolded, page-by-page – an object seemingly inimical to the imagination. But the true meaning that books have for us eludes this logical framework. We pick books up and set them down, begin reading, as we wish; read them partially, or not at all; neglect and give them away. Reading is not constant: the way we read, as a culture and as individuals, alters with time.

Hans Waanders' book intervention in W. H. Hudson's classic study, *Birds of La Plata*, is a beautiful example of a transformed reading. The motif of the kingfisher appears in all of Hans' work, which combines scientific observation, experience and intuition, in an interweaving of the ordering and poetic faculties. Adopting the habits and methods of librarians and bird watchers, Hans published, each year, a *Field Guide* listing the species (title), range (edition), and distinguishing characteristics (contents) of his ouevre. This cataloguing has an obsessive aspect, but one that is redeemed by the generosity and aery play of the imagination that accompanies it. For instance, the most recent includes a found text adapted from a 1950s Field Guide:

> Books can fly where they want to when they want to. So it seems to us, who are earthbound. They symbolise a degree of freedom that we would nearly give our souls to have. Perhaps that is why book watching has almost become a national hobby ... This small book was written for those who have never had a book guide before, but who are becoming aware of the multitude of books with which we live.

It is in the *use* we make of them, not only in reading but in the reassuring and inspiring presence that they have, that books discover their full meaning. *The Libraries of Thought and Imagination* responds to the subtle and shifting character that this meaning has by presenting a new proprioception of the book.

In the modern era, writing, reading and the book have been transformed and the rationalism of print challenged. Successive generations of the avant-garde have developed new models of consciousness and new conceptions of the structure of visual and written language. These have in turn re-shaped book design and typography – an obvious example being Concrete poetry. The process is symbiotic: Thought cannot be separated from Imagination. The philosophy of the book – of Jakobson, Blanchot or Barthes – cannot be separated from the poetry of the book – of Khlebnikov, Olson or Jabès.

Small presses and poet and artist publishers effected a revolution with their wilful, adventurous and untutored approach to publishing. They took possession of all of the possibilities that print technology offered – from offset litho, letterpress, photocopiers, mimeo printers, to typewriters, letraset and rubber-stamps. The attitude of this disparate community is summed up by Robert Creeley: 'For me, and the other writers who came to be involved, it was a place defined by our own activity and accomplished altogether by ourselves ...' Whether in the mass editions of Mayakovsky and El Lizzitsky, small poetry presses and magazines, or in artists' books – however catalogued and shelved – the vivid investigative energy of these publications defines an entire era. These individuals worked with little expectation of audience or profit and established a model that was repeated in the self-publishing strategies of experimental composers, musicians, and film-makers, Punk being a prime example.

I grew up in a cottage heated by heavy storage heaters and insulated by book-lined walls. New books arrived daily, in parcels addressed to my father, covered with exotic stamps: Kyoto, Mexico City, New York, Vienna.

Books were the common currency of friendship. Books were the news. Exploring this poet's library I discovered City Lights Pocketbooks, Cape Editions, Something Else Press; Coracle, Trigram and Moschatel; *Poor.Old.Tired.Horse*, *Aggie Weston's*, *Roy Rodgers*, *Chocolate News*; books by Gertrude Stein, Jackson Mac Low, Louis Zukofsky, the Noigrandres poets and Wien Gruppe.

I immediately wanted to belong to this community of itinerants, enthusiasts and eccentrics. I began by selling a few of the rarer titles to poetry dealers such as Alan Halsey and Peter Riley, who continue to play such a key role. They are part of a great circulatory system – poets, artists, publishers, booksellers and collectors who together form an economy, quite separate from the established book trade. Despite being a community apart which, as Creeley suggests, was self-defined, many of those involved became acutely sensitive to the conventions and idioms of publication and book distribution. Their work pioneered new models of consciousness but it also showed an enthusiasm for how the work found its way in the world. John Calder's involvement in the Paperback Bookshop in Edinburgh, or Sol LeWitt's in Printed Matter Bookstore in New York being two examples.

The most exciting and enduring practitioners presented their work as a library, offering their audience the opportunity to subscribe to a new vision of the world. Take, for instance, Cape Editions edited by the poet Nathaniel Tarn, which published the poet-revolutionaries – Breton, Neruda, Olson – and new thinkers – Levi-Strauss, Barthes – of the 1960s, alongside apparent strays, such as *Bees: Their Vision, Chemical Senses and Language*, by Karl von Frisch. There is an ambition in such projects that takes on a darker aspect in Douglas Gordon's mirror-library, imposed on a collector. The libraries define regions of the imagination reminiscent of those discovered by Sartre in the *Grand Larousse*. It is also true that some of the most famous small presses relate back to real artistic 'Republics' such as Black Mountain College, Deuchar Mill or Little Sparta.

Ian Hamilton Finlay's Wild Hawthorn Press functions in this way, producing pastoral publications for Little Sparta – calendars, postcards, jam-jar labels – and propaganda – letterheads, proclamations, invectives and posters – for the Saint-Just Vigilantes. People who collect his work often feel that they have a special access to the garden, as if the publications were product of a cottage economy, of sheets stitched after tea around the hearth.

For some of the small presses such twilight scenes are familiar. Through the process of making, these publishers gained a new awareness of the proprioception of the book – of how reading is absorbed through the body as much as the mind. Two artists who are deeply involved in the process of making and disseminating are Helen Douglas and Telfer Stokes, who, as Weproductions, have published more than twenty titles (1972-2001). Helen describes how

> From quite early on I felt it wasn't just a book, it was a practice in relation to book ... Through an identification with the book I have been able to give myself to its exploration, it in turn giving itself to my searches, giving shape to my journeys. The book's tangible physical form, its open/closed and sequential structure, together with its established relationship to print and reproduction enables me to make concrete the narrative within me ... The finality of the gathered pages, threaded signatures and bound book guillotined to its final shape embodies for me these moments of completeness within the continuum.

The 'continuum' of meaning extends into the life that a book has in the world. Telfer relates how in the early 1970s he placed a copy of his latest book on the shelf of a London bookshop, then asked an assistant if they, "had a copy of Telfer Stokes' *Passage* in stock", the assistant replying, helpfully, "No, I don't think so, sir, but I will check on the shelves." This visual book did not belong within any recognised category of the trade, but had now been insinuated within the mainstream. Telfer's books make playful reference to publishing idioms: some disguise themselves as paperbacks; on one he paints the cover Pelican blue; on another a 'dog-ear' appears in the upper corner; and on all of them appears the Weproductions logo, Woody the cat. Telfer's story is typical of the democratic idealism of the time, where the book offered an egalitarian alternative to the preciousness of the art object. The innovations of the artist or visual book have been absorbed over time and as new approaches to book design and editing emerge so the catagories themselves are eroded. The pocketbooks project is part of this process.

For me the book revolution is *the* great adventure of the Modern era. Yet it remains true that the book is a naturally conservative form. Consequently, this anthology is not restricted to experimentalism: rather it presents a range of work suggesting the new consciousness of 'book'. The form is so familiar, and so concealed, but in works as dramatic as Nathan Coley's 'Reading Robert Burns to the Scott Monument, Edinburgh, 1999', or Hermione Wiltshire's 'and when I got there', this camouflage is thrown off. The first part of this anthology presents a series of 'Bookshelves' selected by writers and visual artists. These treat the bookshelf as a form, one which discusses diverse subjects, and in which the relation of bibliography to a text or image supplies a unifying framework. Beyond these 'Bookshelves' are ranged a selection of works of visual art, prose and poetry; artist projects, interventions and essays – an index of the libraries of Thought and Imagination.

Bibliography

Clay, Steve, *A Secret Location on the Lower East Side:adventures in writing 1960–1980*, Granary Books, New York, 1998

Clay, Steve & Rotherberg, Jerome, *The Book of the Book,* Granary Books, New York, 2000

Courtney, Cathy, *Speaking of Book Art*, Anderson-Lovelace, Los Altos Hills, CA, 1999

Creeley, Robert, *The Black Mountain Review (1954–57)*, AMS Reprint, 1969

Douglas, Helen, & Stokes, Telfer, Weproductions, 1974–2001

Finlay, Ian Hamilton, Wild Hawthorn Press, 1961–2001

Lauf, Cornelia & Phillpot, Clive, *Artist/Author: Contemporary Artists' Books*, Distributed Art Publishers Inc., New York, 1998

Sartre, Jean-Paul, *Les Mots/The Words*, translated by Irene Clephane, Penguin Books, London, 1964

Waanders, Hans, *Field Guide to the Books of Hans Waanders*, Hans Waanders, Den Bosch, 7th impression, 2001

Williams, William Carlos, 'Asphodel, that greeny flower' in *Pictures from Breughel*, MacGibbon & Keys, 1963

"Ask the Librarian . . ."

A preamble concerning the 'atmospheres' of colour, height and subject

"*Is there a dark red book, about seven-inches tall, defining via examples, the various ways of arranging and ordering books on a bookshelf?*"

The first collection of books that I can recall as a singular *accumulation* – that is to say, a selection gathered together as a 'resource' for a particular concern – was a glass-fronted cabinet containing several shelves of books on the subject of physical geography. This was housed in the corner of a school classroom devoted to the teaching of the geography curriculum, at 'ordinary' (11–16 year-olds) and 'advanced' (16–18 year-olds) levels. Open access to the books in the cabinet was granted to those studying at the advanced level, encouraged by the code, that "knowledge is not remembering facts, but knowing where to find them" – an endorsement of both the inquisitive motivation of the auto-didactically inclined, and of the practical advisory role of the librarian.

My own 'use' of the books in this small and specialised annex to the main school library consisted usually of 'flicking-through-looking-at-the-pictures'. As I recall, most of the books were published in the period of mid-nineteenth century up until the 1960s, and while only being able to remember a few particular titles, I can vividly recall the tone and atmosphere that surrounded the collection (or at least, my impression of the collection). Several titles were from the Collins 'New Naturalist' series, mainly published in the 1950s, with their (then) high-quality colour plates; often of strange colour balance, curiously retouched skies, and sometimes distressingly out-of-register printing. There were books that dealt with the subject of 'fieldwork', describing a didactic purpose and methodology of observation 'out-and-about' in the landscape. Memorably, one or two of these field study titles were illustrated with topographical line drawings, where the line of the landscape and the hand-rendered textual 'legends' were wholly integrated. As drawings they sought to dispense a particular function, acting as an aid to the understanding and 'reading' of the landscape, as opposed to depiction for *artistic* purposes – the brevity of these compositions more like transcription than impression.

During the twenty-five or so years since I last examined this collection of books, I have bought copies of many of the titles for depositing amongst our own bookshelves, not as a distilled *memento* of that selection, but as separate parts of a broader and *active* personal collection. For instance, books by the topographical illustrator Geoffrey Hutchings sit occasionally next door to childrens' books illustrated by Edward Ardizzone – near contemporaries, but draughtsmen of conflicting purpose. Similarly, whereas titles from the 'New Naturalist' series would ordinarily be placed within their own subject category – birds with birds, botany with botany, etc.; my half-dozen or so are placed together as a uniform group, the meaning and purpose being that they represent and illustrate a particular historic *manner* of publishing, both editorially (as a series) and physically (as uniform objects). The coexistent, and equally justifiable logic of both of these systems of categorisation – by subject, or by type – suggests that there are, in effect, always two (or more) possible versions of order using one and the same thing. One of the 'more' versions being the possibility of practical *dis*-order: manifest paradoxically in the *apparent* order of a shelf of mixed-category books arranged by height or colour.

I remember noting at an early age, that to search amongst the shelves of the junior library for a book on a particular subject, might present only an incomplete selection of the available holdings; a further gathering of 'oversize' books could be examined elsewhere. Certain areas of illustrated non-fiction dominate these shelves: art, natural history, regional geography, etc.; while fiction is published almost entirely in 'normal-size' formats – apart from 'large-type' versions for the hard-of-seeing, who usually have their own library-within-a-library. The practical reasoning behind this segregation by format, is of course to avoid over-height shelving for under-height books; that books of the maximum height would determine the gaps between shelves, leaving irregular and wasteful airspace above the more common, smaller formats.

Another segregation, in the larger public libraries is the 'stack', a sometimes mysterious holding of older titles, again arranged subject-by-subject, but often requiring permission to be examined. It is as if both a historical and a geographical boundary exists between the holdings in the stack and those currently in the main body of the lending library. Given that in most public libraries there is an optimum number of titles that can practically be available at any time, and as new titles are acquired, the notional break-off point moves chronologically forward. Books that I examined in the stack of my local town library in the 1970s, that had been published in the 1930s and 1940s, would now have been joined by titles from the 1960s and 1970s; then part of the active lending library. The notable difference between the stack and the current, is therefore one of age – that the books in the stack contain *old* or out-of-date information, superseded by newer publications on the same subject held elsewhere. Books on outmoded subjects would certainly be found in the stack – technical works about radio involving glass valves, for instance; or books on geology and earth science unwittingly absent of any mention of 'plate tectonics' – while the majority of books required no justification or excuse for having been published thirty or more years earlier. However, with the problems of differentiating that which is still definitive or current from what is not, this demarcation and grouping based on publication date is the most logical and reasonable slimming-down method for an expanding holding of titles.

Very few people would divide their own books into pre- and post-a particular publication date; and very few people – apart perhaps from professional librarians – arrange the books in their homes according to the Dewey Decimal System. Further, unlike a public library, very few people actually possess collections of books that range across the scope of subjects defined by such a complete system. The most common, the *average* domestic collection of books, is probably imbalanced towards fiction and novels, and these might be arranged alphabetically by author; or chronologically, as read (the earliest sometimes separated as a personal 'stack'); or by publisher (the old orange-spined Penguin, the green-spined Virago) or genre (crime, horror, romance, etc.); or not arranged particularly at all. In addition, a non-fictional interest might form another grouping that would demand a practical placing within the house – recipe books, for example, housed separately in the kitchen or dining room; and if extensive, by country or course: Indian, Italian, soups or desserts. Likewise, erotica might find its most comfortable location in the bedroom, while the lavatorial reader is a niche-genre of its own.

In our house the shelves in the downstairs front room contain books on art, history, literature, music, philosophy, etc. – broadly cultural sub-jects. While in the back room, there are books on birds, gardening, geog-raphy, weather, etc. – the natural world, as such. The division is as much practical as it is thematic; the quantity of books divided with the bulk (and also the bigger, but not necessarily 'oversize' ones) in the front room. However, the classifications described above are not always definite – there being no need for them to be – and therefore anomalies and what might seem to be misplacings are many. Because it is a house, for living and working in, and the books are for using day-to-day, rather than a library or office primarily for study or work, there is no imperative for a system of ordering and grouping beyond a *familiar* active use.

For instance, a public library will usually separate the titles of local interest into a 'local studies' section, whereas our 'local' books are by subject, whether they are to do with topography, or architecture.

Upstairs, in what purports to be an office, there is another accumulation of books and printed material that is shelved, or piled, without any obvious logic or arrangement: source material, and books of miscellaneous subjects that are of particular interest in terms of design and format and production; catalogues and lists; typographical specimen books and material samples; dictionaries and other reference books. Common to this type of *singularly* practical, but seemingly haphazard collection of material, is the ability of the owner – or *home librarian* – to locate anything almost instantly.

A further distinction is often made between the already housed and the freshly acquired. In a public library new books will initially await the procedures and devices of registration, then to be shelved and labelled for a short period as 'new acquisitions'. Domestically, the new and as yet *unread* might be grouped together, in some cases perhaps as 'trophies', but generally in anticipation of being both started and finished. The book-laden coffee-table presents a complexion of the owners current interests, inasmuch as an entire collection offers a compounded view of previous interests – a *historic* complexion; although parts missing by 'de-acquisition' will present a manipulated and partial view. (It is an unusually stable individual that chooses to consistently resist the temptation to pare at an accumulation of books – to adopt a policy of complete acceptance of all past reading.) Consciously or not, the ownership of bookshelves is a constantly active licence for addition, arrangement and removal – the processes of *editing* inherent in the making of books themselves.

Colin Sackett

Bookshelves

Alec Finlay

Ultra Crepidam

Graham Fagen

Ultra Crepidam

I was invited to make use of his town house while he was away in the Hebrides. He had posted me his spare set of keys – this was fortunate, as finding appropriate lodgings in the expensive city was the cause of my angst. So I was grateful. It was the end of August, the light would be perfect, a liquid gloss, that if you looked hard to see and understand, resulted in you having to blink for a few seconds.

His house was neat. The spare bed had been made up in the study. A south-facing room – plenty of light. Pale blue walls, not cold though. A warm blue, contemplative. One wall white. Shelves with files, desk with computer, printer, that sort of thing. Recess shelves with books, video tapes in plain cases and wee slide boxes.

I sat at the end of the bed next to the clean towels that had been left for me. As I let my bag drop I noticed a small pile of books on the floor at the foot of the bed. Peculiar. Not fitting in with the tidy order of the room at all. I reached down. The book on top wasn't a book but a photocopy of one. I picked it up and read the first page.

> The historian cannot help dividing his material into 'periods,' nicely defined in the *Oxford Dictionary* as 'distinguishable portions of history.' To be distinguishable, each of these portions has to have a certain unity; and if the historian wishes to verify this unity instead of merely pre-supposing it, he must needs try to discover intrinsic analogies between such overtly disparate phenomena as the arts, literature, philosophy, social and political currents, religious movements, etc. This effort, laudable and even indispensable in itself, has led to a pursuit of 'parallels' the hazards of which are only too obvious. No man can master more than one fairly limited field; every man has to rely on incomplete and often secondary information when ever he ventures *ultra crepidam*.

This opening paragraph had me deep in thought. Not understanding the Latin phrase at the end I imagined what it could mean.

The next book *was* a book. Hard bound. Heavy. It was full of maps and graphic diagrams, plans and models, facts and figures. Black and white photographs of current buildings juxtaposed next to fantastic images of what could be.

The Plan

Concept

8.20 Having set out growth targets for the development of the New Town, and appraised the existing conditions and the physical requirements of the new population related to the objectives set out in paragraph 8.13, the urban structure plan was drawn up on the basis of an examination of the relationships between land use, transportation and urban form.

The pages were glossy and the information seemed right. This book knew what it was about. A single subject. I put it down because of its weight.

The book now at the top of the pile was small with a black and white picture of a man on the cover. A worn receipt marked a place. It was the notes. I glanced at a few.

9. *peach*: inform.
26. *for a cod*: for a joke.
67. *whiteboy*:
72. fenian movement ...
79. *fecked*: stolen.
80. *scut*: ran away.
93. *twice nine*: nine strokes on each hand.
23. *les jupes*: French for 'skirts.'
25. *a muff*: a beginner.
28. *Victor Hugo*: (1802-85), dominant figure in French Romanticism.

I closed the book to look at the cover again. *Portrait of the Artist as a Young Man*. I looked hard at the face of the man on the cover. His head leaning slightly to his right. I looked at his clothes. A flat cap on his head.

Dark jacket, light trousers. There was a greenhouse behind him. A window was opened and a flower could be seen in the gap. It was in a pot, it looked like a ceramic pot. I knew what it would smell like to stand there. Then I went on to the next book.

The cover was much brighter, curvy lines and a strange man looking tense but excited at the same time. I opened the book at random. It was immediately apparent from the format that it was some sort of script.

	Shot of Crackers, lying nude on his bed, surrounded by chicken corpses.
EDIE	Babs, where do eggs come from?
BABS	From little chickens, Mama. They lay them and we eat them.
EDIE	But suppose someday there weren't any chickens. Would that mean there wouldn't be any eggs?

I turned to another page.

MUFFY	A Chihuahua, Mole?
MOLE	No, you'll see – close your eyes! (*She does*) No peeking now! (*She takes down pants*)
MUFFY	Hurry, Mole! The suspense is killing me!
MOLE	You can open 'em now.
MUFFY	(*Opens eyes and sees hideous phony sex-change penis*) Ahhhhhhhhhh!!! (*Falling backwards, gagging*) What have you done to yourself?!?
MOLE	(*Advancing*) I got the sex change just for you, Muffy. (*Tries to hump her*)

I looked at the black and white picture of the action and laughed to myself. I thought, what the hell's this about? Guilt made me shut the book and put it down while picking up the next one.

It was a small thick book, with the image of a man's face taking up the whole of the front cover. I recognised it immediately. Robert Burns. A piece of paper stuck out from the page I had opened the book at. On the paper was a hand written note.

Jamaica pages: 143, 153, 161, 166, 282, 324, 325.

I skimmed the pages of the open book.

> Clarinda was going to Jamaica! She was sailing in February in the *Roselle* – the very ship in which he had meant to embark if he had failed of his Edinburgh edition.

Judging by the covers, the two books that were under this one dealt more directly with Jamaica. The first was a book of short stories about the Island. The other was a history of Jamaican music.

I laughed when looking at the contents page of the book of stories.

WHY DEM CALL U-ROY, U-ROY
TREE BAD GAL
DROGS BIZNIS
TUFFEE AVE A VISION

Then I thought, why don't I laugh at the spelling in Burns poetry? Why do I find reading Burns hard and reading this easy?

After reading some of the lyrics in the book of Jamaican music I wondered if there was a link between Burns and these contemporary songs. Was this what my absent host was thinking too? Scottish people who had left home for Jamaica. The trade. Imperialism. Could that have been the reason why these three books were next to each other?

I remembered that he was in Jamaica a few months before. The unnerving feeling of following the thoughts of someone else intensified when I glanced down at the last book in the pile. This book was about the Hebrides. The place where my host was. I was sitting in his house, browsing his books. The ones he had left on the floor at the end of my bed, his spare bed.

As I flicked through the pages I realised it was a book about a journey, which eventually ended up in the Hebrides. More than that, it was a diary account, written by the two traveling companions. It was about them and about the country they were in. Both were inextricably linked but separate too.

Bibliography

Panofsky, Erwin, *Gothic Architecture and Scholasticism*, Meridian Books, New York, 1957

Irvine Development Corporation, *Irvine New Town Plan*, Irvine Development Corporation, Irvine, Scotland, 1971

Joyce, James, *Portrait of the Artist as a Young Man*, Penguin, London, 1914-15

Waters, John, *Trash Trio*, Fourth Estate, London, 1989

Carswell, Catherine, *The Life of Robert Burns*, Canongate Books, Edinburgh, 1930

Kennaway, Guy, *One People*, Canongate Books, Edinburgh, 1997

Chang, Kevin O'Brien & Chen, Wayne, *Reggae Routes: The Story of Jamaican Music*, Ian Randle Publishers, Kingston, Jamaica, 1998

Johnson, Samuel & Boswell, James, *Journey to the Hebrides*, Canongate Books (Canongate Classics), Edinburgh, 1996

A Kurt Schwitters Bookshelf

The spines depicted here belong to Schwitters monographs
held in the Glasgow School of Art library.

David Bellingham, 1995

iters

Museum des 20. Jahrhunderts, Wien

KURT SCHWITTERS (1887–1948)

Untitled (*For the Birds*)

On 1 May 2000, I was thinking about the American composer John Cage and wanted to gather more material on his work. As I often do in these situations, I visited the Amazon site and, though I was looking for a specific collection of interviews, decided to see what else was available and so performed a general search typing, simply, 'John Cage'.

Obviously, a great deal of material was found during the search, although when I came to look at the list of books, many of those initially suggested seemed to be about the keeping of birds, an activity with which I had not associated the composer. I was aware of his fascination with ecological matters generally, and mushrooms in particular, but this was one area of his interests which had escaped my attention altogether. It was at this point that I realised that all the avarian publications were written by men named 'John'; of course, all the books were concerned with the keeping of caged birds. The title I was looking for was out of print. I ordered four of the other publications instead.

I found a copy of Cage's interviews, *For the Birds*, a few weeks later in a London bookshop.

Bibliography

Bales, John, *Guide to Owning an Amazon Parrot*, TFH Publications, Neptune City, NJ, 1997

Cage, John, *For the Birds*, Marion Boyars, London, 1981

Coborn, John, *Cockatoos ... as a Hobby*, TFH Publications, Neptune City, NJ, 1994

Harley, John, *Pet Owner's Guide to Cockateil*, Ringpress Books, Lyndney, Glos., 2000

Porter, John, *The Proper Care of Canaries*, TFH Publications, Neptune City, NJ, 1994

Jeremy Millar

Building Books
Bob Arnold

Building Books

Of all the tool-boxes yanked from trucks, or automobile trunks, lifted out of back seats, or even carried in as a canvas bag, I never saw a book tucked away in one. A book is about the last thing ever spotted on a job-site, and usually it is a tossed away manual for some equipment. But I read books on the job – sandwich in one hand, Basho in the other – and I'd carry my books in my lunch pail. Because I read, I often earned the nickname 'Preacher'.

So it isn't any accident I still bring books to my building job-sites, now thirty-five years at it and going strong. I started out as a boy carpenter working for my family lumber business and those jobs were mostly modern quick-built homes. A dynamo crew could nail up a half-dozen homes over one summer. I soon moved to Vermont and worked with building crews here or there, but really I worked best alone or with one companion helper. There were countless old homes I worked on, repairing stonework to carpentry. One of my strangest jobs was helping an owner build his large house – mostly I was there to show him how to frame and he would carry on when I had to be away – but his one demand of the house was how he wanted no windows, just a door. Since he lived the greater part of the year at a university job far from his new home, he was wary of vandals and wanted to keep any out by keeping any windows out. That was until I reminded him how vandals could just as easily chainsaw an entry into his house to rummage inside, steel door or not. On hearing that, he agreed to put a few windows in. Small ones. Since this friend was a university librarian, we talked books and writers from sun up to sun down on the job, and then on the long drives he gave me back to my home.

In the year 2000 I began to build a cottage on our land with my fifteen-year-old son, Carson. A two-storey, timber-framed, steel-roofed and wood side-shingled building, boxed out with many windows since

I've been storing salvaged windows from other jobs for years. No better place to draw the daylight and save on wall material. The cottage haunched on a wide stone ledge and was a complete bugger to hand lay dry stone upon, and, under the building frame, but we did. A month long chore. And during that time Carson and I talked music and books and films and even reminisced about the trips we did together as a family on trains, and we also fought and fussed a little because it was hot work and because we are father and son. Building this cottage together – twelve feet wide by eighteen feet long – would be the first leg of Carson's home-school studies. A program that kept him happily away from the local high-school and into percolating sessions of *book learning and back work earning*, as they once used to say.

When Carson asks which books meant the most to me as a builder – including the books I would bring along to jobs as companions – whether they had anything to do with building or not, these are the ones that always spring to mind. A neat dozen. Someday, we'll have these books on a shelf in the cottage when we're done: *Working and Thinking on the Waterfront* by Eric Hoffer (real worker/real writer); *The Long-Legged House* by Wendell Berry (real farmer/real writer); *Payne Hollow* by Harlan Hubbard (husband & wife homesteading quiet team); *The Rock Is My Home* by Werner Blaser (my bible for stone work and its environment); *Indians in Overalls* by Jaime DeAngulo (no better writer to start you at dirt level); *The Granite Pail* by Lorine Niedecker (no better poet for the fine point flowing details); *The Selected Letters of Robinson Jeffers* (who made his west coast days around legends & stone); *The Celtic Twilight* by W. B. Yeats (this could be inter-changed with Synge's *The Aran Islands*: both ultimate, tidy, lunch-pail companions); *The Sign of Jonas* by Thomas Merton (the other ultimate, tidy, lunch-pail companion); *Ian Hamilton Finlay* by Yves Abrioux (in the evening, after work, to sit and visit with this craftsman's world); *A Pattern Language* by Christopher Alexander et al. (no better on towns, buildings, construction worldwide); *The Folk Songs* of North America by Alan Lomax (because there should be a song in your working head).

Now getting older with my bad back blues I've made a new friend in a Chinese gentleman named Dr. Xu. He speaks difficult English but we talk in body gestures and words. And since he knows I'm a builder he has asked me questions about how to fix things. Being fearless, he is a great learner. He shared with me the other day how he put a section of new roofing on his house. He would climb up in short sessions - tucking some shingles under his arm - and bang nails on his one day off each week. He was a little leery of the ladder but his devoted wife held that for him. It wasn't hard at all, he assured me. The first thing he did was to go to his local library to find a book on roofing and its procedures, and then he began.

Bibliography

Hoffer, Eric, *Working and Thinking on the Waterfront*, Harper & Row, 1969

Berry, Wendell, *The Long-Legged House*, Ballantine Paperback, 1971

Harlan Hubbard, *Payne Hollow*, Eakins, 1974

Blaser, Werner, *The Rock is My Home*, Van Nostrand Reinhold, 1976

Angulo, Jaime de, *Indians in Overalls: The Hudson Review Anthology*,
    Frederick Morgan (ed.), Vintage paperback, 1961

Niedecker, Lorine, *The Granite Pail*, Cid Corman (ed.), North Point Press, 1985

Jeffers, Robinson, *The Selected Letters of Robinson Jeffers*, Ann N. Ridgeway (ed.),
    John Hopkins University, 1968

Yeats, W. B., *The Celtic Twilight*, Signet Paperback, 1962

Synge, John, *The Aran Islands*, George Allen and Unwin, 1961

Merton, Thomas, *The Sign of Jonas*, Harcourt, 1953

Abrioux, Yves, *Ian Hamilton Finlay: A Visual Primer*, MIT Press, 1992

Alexander, Christopher, et al., *A Pattern Language*, Oxford University Press, 1977

Lomax, Alan, *The Folk Songs of North America*, Doubleday, 1960

The West
Jane Wodening

The West

There's a place in Southern Utah where a crack goes for thirty miles through the desert and down below inside the crack is a narrow fertile place with a stream and flowers and ruins from Anasazi peoples who lived there on the cliffs in old days. The place is called Grand Gulch and I have been there and will never forget it.

Why then the cleft called Fourth of July is called a Canyon, I don't know, since it's only a glacial gouge seven miles long, from the Continental Divide to the little town of Eldora in the terminal moraine.

Very close to the top of the Fourth of July, in a side valley at timberline, Jim Benedict, a geologist, found stone tools and projectile points from intermittent periods from about three-hundred-and-fifty years ago to nine thousand years ago. Also in that little valley he noted the rock glacier that many times in the past had filled this canyon to nearly a thousand feet deep and presumably will again. He wrote the book, *The Fourth of July Valley: Glacial Geology and Archeology of the Timberline Ecotone.*

The Fourth of July is my canyon where I have lived and wandered for the past ten years. I know the place where the rock glacier sits, innocuous, hardly noticeable. A crashed plane from decades ago is not far away. I have worked with Jim Benedict, digging with great care and had the honour to find a spearpoint made over nine thousand years ago, knapped with exquisite skill.

In the West one can see the geology a lot better because it's dry and the vegetation is small. And naturally I try to understand the rock formations. 'What in Tarnation is *that*?' Sedimentary layers tipped to near vertical, cinder cones, wind-carved stones, balanced rocks, streams that make chasms, streams that don't, chasms with no streams. I can see the dynamic in the shape of the rock. It all seems to be 'inactive at the moment.' 'Geological Time' is a concept difficult for me to encompass.

Coming East from Owens Valley in California across Nevada and Utah I drove first across a pass in California so ancient it had exposed rocks that had been mud when giant primordial worms had squished through it. Down quickly into a flatland with hills ahead of me in the distance then up and over the same again. I had seen this type of land-shape in the Mojave Desert too – had lived on the edge of the Calico Range, looked across the Mojave River Valley (don't think there's water on the surface) to the Newberry Range. Go up the road a ways and there's more valleys and more ranges. John McPhee explains all in *Basin & Range*. Not only very readable but also profound.

When I roamed in the Mojave Desert, I would occasionally see thin trails wavering through the desert and it seemed to me that only humans would leave a trail like that. They would lead to a peak where one could see for miles or perhaps to a beautiful stone that had been carefully flaked into a fascinating but seemingly useless object. These trails were very old, hundreds or – who knew – even thousands of years old.

Carobeth Laird left her anthropologist husband John Peabody Harrington to marry George Laird, a Chemehuevi Indian and couldn't resist taking down his accounts of traditional Chemehuevi life across the twenty-one years of their marriage.

The Chemehuevi Indians lived in the desert with very little in the way of material goods but the main inheritance that went from father to son was the song that told the hunting trails that they could use through the desert.

Carobeth Laird wrote her book, *The Chemehuevis*, in her seventies from a nursing home.

Once I tried to visit Leslie Marmon Silko in the outskirts of Tucson, up a steep and bumpy hill. I knew I was close when I saw her ten-gallon mailbox with lively skeletons painted all over it intertwined with bright colours. After that, skulls and phantoms showed the route and I knew I was at the right house when three dogs attacked the car.

Well, I know dogs pretty well, and besides they couldn't bite me through the car door so since they seemed to be all the attention I got, I talked with them, and befriended the little female with the intelligent eyes. Then Ms. Silko's thirteen-year-old son came home from school and showed me all of their animals, including the albino black snake and the iguanas that were hard to find in the greenhouse. "You should take that dog," he said. "She bites everyone else." I was glad he told me that. I might have taken her. "You'd better go before my mom comes home. She doesn't have time for people."

"Okay, if you say so," I said with regret. I didn't look at the dog as I left for fear I'd take her anyway.

Leslie Marmon Silko has written several books with her people, the Laguna Pueblo Indians, as characters. Any one of the books is very much worth reading. Her *Ceremony* is in the common Native American story-shape of The Quest.

I have met Wallace Black Elk twice on the occasion of his need for a healing sweat lodge. Naturally I called him Grandfather, although he's only fifteen years older than I am. The medicine man, Dave Swallow, younger than me and not related to Wallace, calls him Uncle. Grandfather Wallace tells clearly how the more truly an animal you are, the more spiritual you become. It's obvious on his face. His eyes don't pierce, they simply see, clear inside. And his talk is like that too, amazingly spiritual.

His healing was for a sore on his ankle that wouldn't heal. After four sweat lodges, he was back on his feet and travelling the world with his amazing talk (*Black Elk, The Sacred Ways of a Lakota*).

The History of the Lewis and Clark Expedition seems a good way to say farewell to the Indian books and look at the West through European eyes. Clark actually wrote a dictionary, *The Indian Sign Language*, describing in excruciating detail without pictures the hand movements that were used among the many languages of Native Americans across the continent:

> *Distant* – Bring right hand back to right, in front of right breast, and little lower than shoulder, fingers curved and touching, ball of thumb resting on side of index, hand close to body; push the hand to front, raising it slightly. Very distant indeed would be represented by extending arm to full length.

I have quite a few books on edible plants. My favourite is *Wild Plants of the Pueblo Province: Exploring Ancient and Enduring Uses*, by William W. Dunmire and Gail D. Tierney. It makes me realise that if people were raised to it and were thoughtful about it, they could really live off the land. I used this book a lot in *The Tablets* (as yet unpublished) as my characters wandered through the southwestern deserts.

Hope Ryden, a New Yorker, has written some books of her observations of animal behaviour in the West and *God's Dog: A Celebration of the North American Coyote*, is an amazing book. I used it a lot for my book *Wolf* (which hasn't been published yet either). 'God's dog' is the coyote. People these days call it the 'lowly coyote.' However, Coyotl the Trickster is a major spirit in the North and South American pantheons – very much akin to Loki, Thoth, Hermes, Mercury, or Maui.

One of the wonderful things about the coyote is its adaptability. 'Prairie wolf,' 'bush wolf,' 'desert wolf,' 'mountain wolf.' The big wolf gets exterminated but the coyote adapts.

The best tracker's handbook that I've found talks about history and personality traits as well as eating, mating, habits, moving about, etc. It also mentions all kinds of sign – tracks, marks on trees, bathroom habits – complete with seasonal differences. Also suggests how best to handle encounters and gives glimpses of behaviour. It's called *The Complete Tracker: Tracks, Signs and Habits of North American Wildlife*, by Len McDougall. I have several times sat and read section after section with pleasure as well as using it to understand tracks and signs I find around the canyon. I don't, however, track – partly to leave wild folks alone with their private lives, but also because I get pulled away along the way by distractions too numerous to mention.

My very favourite western hero for all time is Hugh Glass. As a role model, he is unbeatable. Although leadership was not his trump suit, scouting and most particularly survival were. The one great occasion that showed his mettle was that on which he was horribly mauled by a bear and left for dead two hundred miles from anywhere and managed to crawl about half that distance then make a raft and arrived at the Fort fat and sassy enough for anyone's taste.

Frederick Manfred who spent weeks exploring the area that Hugh Glass crawled, also, in *Lord Grizzly*, describes Glass' environment – the efforts to conquer the Indians, the various leaders and life at the Forts, the other people around, several of whom have become more famous than Hugh Glass.

When I moved to this canyon, I had just finished reading *Lord Grizzly* for perhaps the third time so that when my family cried out – "You have no neighbours and no telephone! What if you break a leg? You'll have to crawl three miles!" I snapped my fingers at them, at the thought of crawling three miles with a broken leg. But I did go ahead and get into ham radio anyway.

I find Jack London's short story 'To Light a Fire' as close to the heart as the long crawl of Hugh Glass. With that and his *Call of the Wild*, he must join my pantheon.

Colorado: A Literary Chronicle, edited by W. Storrs Lee, was recommended to me by Ed Dorn and I tremendously enjoy dipping into it. It is an exceptional collection of exquisite (and otherwise) literati variously faced with the reality of the patch of land called Colorado. *The Outlaw Years: The History of the Land Pirates of The Natchez Trace*, by Robert M. Coates (another Ed Dorn recommendation) covers that interesting time in Western history, centred on Tombstone, as many of the outlaws were. *The Moffat Road* is a beautiful book with lots of pictures showing how the trains moved across the land, tamed it and took it. In my childhood I lived close to the Burlington Route and loved to hear it howling. Now in the Fourth of July I can hear it still when the wind is right.

When I came down from having just climbed Longs Peak in 1977, I went about saying, "It was six hours of terror!" My friend Huntley said, "That's just what Isabella Bird said about climbing Longs Peak in 1906!"

Isabella Bird was an English lady who was always ill in England, but was one very tough lady when she travelled. When she came to the Rockies, she spent a winter a few miles north of here at the foot of Longs Peak, ultimately recording it all in *A Lady's Life in the Rocky Mountains*.

In Charles Olson's *Call Me Ishmael*, Olson never names the Rocky Mountains per se but he obsesses on SPACE from every direction. 'SPACE ... the central fact to man born in America ... It is geography at bottom.' He seems convinced that something in the shape of the land itself sets people against nature. 'It was not the will to be free but the will to overcome nature that lies at the bottom of us as individuals and a people.' 'Like Ahab, American, one aim: lordship over nature.' This pains me deeply but as I look around me I cannot say it isn't so. It seems to be very vigorously so today.

Two books written about a century apart I'd like to pair up as a finale – Mark Twain's *Roughing It* and Jack Keroac's *On the Road*. The two explore two very different worlds but the same general area of land – The West.

Bibliography

Benedict, James B., *The Fourth of July Valley: Glacial Geology and Archeology of the Timberline Ecotone*, Center for Mountain Archeology, Ward, CO, 1981

McFee, John, *Basin & Range*, Farrar, Strauss & Giroux, 1981

Laird, Carobeth, *The Chemehuevis*, Malki Museum Press, Morongo Indian Reservation, Banning, CA, 1976

Silko, Leslie Marmon, *Ceremony*, Viking Penguin, 1977

Black Elk, Wallace, & Lyon, William S., *Black Elk, The Sacred Ways of a Lakota*, Harper, 1991

Coues, Elliot (ed), *The History of the Lewis and Clark Expedition*, Volumes 1–3 (unabridged), Constable & Co., Dover, 1979

Clark, W. P., *The Indian Sign Language*, University of Nebraska Press, 1982

Dunmire, W. W., & Tierney G D., *Wild Plants of the Pueblo Province: Exploring Ancient and Enduring Uses*, Museum of New Mexico Press, Santa Fe, NM, 1995

Ryden, Hope, *God's Dog: A Celebration of the North American Coyote*, Penguin, 1979

McDougall, Len, *The Complete Tracker: Tracks, Signs and Habits of North American Wildlife*, The Lyons Press, 1997

Manfred, Frederick, *Lord Grizzly*, Signet, 1954

Labor, Earle, (ed.), *The Portable Jack London*, Penguin, 1994

Lee, W. Storrs, (ed.), *Colorado: A Literary Chronicle*, Funk & Wagnalls, 1970

Coates, Robert M., *The Outlaw Years: The History of the Land Pirates of The Natchez Trace*, The Literary Guild of America, 1930

The Moffat Road Bollinger & Bauer Sage Books, Denver, 1962

Bird, Isabella, *A Lady's Life in the Rocky Mountains*, University of Oklahoma Press, 1985

Twain, Mark, *Roughing It*, Signet, 1962

Keroac, Jack, *On the Road,* Signet, 1957

Book Mountain

Bibliography

Walpole, Hugh, *Portrait of a Man with Red Hair*, Daily Express Fiction Library,
    London, n.d.

Ayres, Ruby M., *Missing the Tide*, Hodder & Stoughton, London, 1952

Fairless, Michael, *The Roadmender*, Collin's Clear-Type Press,
    London and Glasgow, n.d.

Shute, Nevil, *The Far Country*, The Book Club, London, 1953

Magness, T. A., *Hill of the Jackals*, Blackie & Son, London, 1953

Leyland, Eric & Scott-Chard, T. E., *Comet Round the World*,
    Hunter Hawk Series No.5, Edmund Ward, London, 1959

Prole, Lozania *Our Dearest Emma*, The Book Club, London, n.d.

Atkins, G. Glenn, *From the Hillside*, Independent Press, London, 1948
    N. B. This has a handwritten poem inside it by AJW on a separate sheet

Wilson, T. W., *What Happened to Kitty*, Blackie & Son, London and Glasgow, n.d.

Jones, Timothy Angus, *The Small Hours of the Night*, James Barrie, London, 1925

Carr, E. H., *International Relations Between The Two Wars 1919–1939*,
    MacMillan & Co, St Martin's Press, New York

Dickens, Charles, *David Copperfield*, The Thames Publishing Co., London, n.d.

Parkinson, C. Northcote, *In-Laws and Outlaws*, John Murray, London, 1962

Warren, C. Henry, *Miles from Anywhere,* Eyre & Spottiswoode, London, 1948

Berna, Paul, *They Didn't Come Back*, The Bodley Head, London, 1969

Basling, Tom, *The Olympic Sleeper*, Eyre Methuen, London, 1979

Pape, Richard, *Boldness Be My Friend*, Elek, London, 1953

Sudell, Richard, *Practical Home Gardening*, Odhams Press Ltd, London, 1949

Vanbrugh, Irene, *To Tell My Story*, Hutchinson & Co, London, 1949

Hutton, Edward, *The Life of Christ in the Old Italian Masters*, Chatto & Windus,
    London, 1935

Business Procedures for the Small Building Firm, Comprint Ltd, London, n.d.

Hamish Fulton, 1997

The Little Wild Goose Pagoda
Peter McCarey

The Little Wild Goose Pagoda

'He arrived at the frontier gates of death carrying the melons on his head.'

I tried to put it back on the shelf and leave it but I really couldn't not buy that: *Monkey* by Wu Ch'eng-ên, translated by Arthur Waley, 'BOOK PRODUCTION WAR STANDARD ECONOMY', £2.50 from Voltaire and Rousseau in Glasgow.

I liked those wartime editions partly because I could afford them, partly for the poignancy of people reading in the blackout. I've never bought a book because it was a first edition or because it was a beautiful object. Blame the Vatican and the Kremlin. The book is the wrapping; the Word's the thing. In the USSR the handsomely bound efforts were Brezhnev, Leonid, opera omnia. Anything worthwhile circulated in the barter system on the usual cheap paper. My Gaelic books got me a set of Blok's poems and a cruel hangover.

But some things just weren't available: Shestov, for instance. Even in the year the Soviets were publishing Mandelshtam, Lev Isaakovich was invisible, in the central libraries but not in the catalogues. I know he was there because I saw a young librarian reading him in a café near the Academy of Sciences Library: she'd taken it from the secret stacks. Does this sound like *The Name of the Rose*? It should, because printing does not guarantee survival. Nor does the writing. A work's survival depends entirely on the individual reader. And as for the bookshelf – the more important a book becomes the more you realise you don't own it at all: you're looking after it.

The Soviets were afraid of books: afraid of letting them in, afraid of letting them out. It took time to get permission to leave with books I'd brought with me to Leningrad, and a big official stamp was put on the last printed page of Edwin Morgan's translations of Mayakovsky; same for Dante's *Inferno*, whose last canto now ends with an exit visa from the Soviet Ministry of Culture.

If heaven is a bookshelf, hell is a book. Choose carefully . You might find yourself in 'Russia's War' by Richard Overy, or in *Malcolm Caldwell's South-East Asia*. You might find yourself selling them all for bread, your pension not worth tuppence. Which is still better than living on the street in Manila.

Bookish fears of the well-to-do become encysted and transfigured on the right side of the law: to break the law is wrong but to gain from it is surely sinful. Solution? Posit something infinitely worse than hell on earth to paralyse the conscience.

My bookshelf is blessed with a

HAND BOOK OF
CHINESE BUDDHISM
BEING
SANSKRIT-CHINESE
DICTIONARY
WITH
VOCABULARIES OF BUDDHIST TERMS
in Pali, Singhalese, Siamese, Burmese,
Tibetan, Mongolian and Japanese
ERNEST J. EITEL
SECOND EDITION
REVISED AND ENLARGED

prefaced in Hongkong, March 1888, reprinted Madras 1992.

I use a lot of odd dictionaries, some of which, if you were to sling them in a pond, would mushroom into so many second-hand bookshops, the proprietor hunched over a calor gas stove in the corner, perishing from black lung, and a plastic sheet under the leaky roof bellying with bathfuls of rainwater, an accident waiting to happen; a dozen hapless browsers immortalised in papier-maché while consulting: L. Levitchi, *Dictionar Romîn-Englez* (Bucharest, 1960) – '*joian* s.m. name given to an ox born on a Thursday'; *Brewer's Dictionary of Phrase and Fable* – the entry on the Duke of Argyll; *Dorland's Medical Dictionary*, 24th ed. – 'NOTE – an *infusion* flows in by gravity, an *injection* is forced in by a syringe, an *instillation* is dropped in, an *insufflation* is blown in and an *infection* slips in unnoticed'; a dictionary of Russian prison camp slang which, for empty prattle, gives the elaborate 'discussing the effects of lunar rays on herpes in the hereafter'.

Eitel, though, is in a class of his own. His entry for 'Nâraka' has to be seen in its enormity:

NÂRAKA (Pâli. Miraya. Siam. Narok. Burm. Niria. Tib. Myalba. Mong. Tamu) . . . explained by . . . (nara) . . . (ka), lit. men's wickedness, or by . . . lit. unenjoyable, or by . . . lit. instruments of torture; or . . . (Niraya) explained by . . . lit. prison under the earth, or by . . . lit. the prefecture of darkness. General term for the various divisions of hell. (1.) The hot hells . . . eight of which (see Samdjiva, Kâlasûtra, Samghata, Râurava, Mahârâurava, Tapana, Tratâpana, and Avîtchi) are situated underneath Djambudvîpa in tiers, beginning at a depth of 11,900 yôdjanas, and reach to a depth of 40,000 yôdjanas; but as each of these hells has four gates and outside each gate four antechamber-hells, there are altogether 136 hot hells. (2.) The cold hells . . . eight in number (see Arbuda, Nirarbuda, Atata, Hahava, Ahaha, Utpala, Padma and Pundarîka), situated under-neath the two Tchakravâlas and ranging shaft-like one beneath the other, but so that this shaft is gradually widening down to the fourth hell and then narrowing again, the first and last hells having the shortest and the fourth hell the longest diameter. (3.) The dark hells, eight in number, sit-uated between the two Tchakravâlas; also called vivifying hells . . . because any being, dying in the first of these hells, is at once reborn in the second, and so forth, life lasting 500 years in each of these hells.

(4.) The cold Lôkântarika hells (lit. hells on the edge sc. of the universe), ten in number, but each having 100 millions of smaller hells attached, all being situated outside of the Tchakravâlas. (5.) The 84,000 small Lôkântarika hells (lit. small hells on the edge), divided into three classes, as situated on mountains, or on water, or in deserts. Each universe has the same number of hells, distributed so that the northern continent contains no hell at all, the two continents E. and W. of the Mêru have only the small Lôkântarika hells, and all the other hells are situated under the southern continent (Djambudvîpa). There are different torments in the different hells; the length of life also differs in each class of hells; *but the distinctions made are too fanciful to be worth enumerating.*

My italics. It goes on, though, and ends with a special hell for females: '(lit. placenta tank), consisting of an immense pool of blood. From this hell, it is said, no release is possible'.

Clearly, the former Soviet Union is the cold hells, the former Zaire the hot and Nâraka itself is governed from Bretton Woods. Back to the bookshelf. What is it with books? Why are most of them novels and biographies and cookery? Do people really have to be spoonfed? It's true that a novel can take my mind off squabbles with other bureaucrats, but in almost everything I read I find myself checking how many pages are left till I'm done with it. The last big exception to that was Nicolas Bouvier's *l'Usage du monde* (in English *The Way of the World*) and it was, of all things, a travel book. Most travel books seem designed to endorse the reader's prejudice or laziness. This one had me champing at the bit, wanting to take off now for the East. The author's father was head of the Geneva Public and University Library, whose utmost stacks and incunabulae – Scottish universities take note – are available to the reading public of the city. It's where I borrowed a copy of Athanasius Kircher's *China*, when I got back from Xi'an – city of the T'ang poets, who knew that government and the law existed to make room for music and verse. In the 'Forest of Steles', where the classics and historical documents are engraved in stone, I got a calque of a poem:

> Moon down, crows up, sky of frost
> River trees, fishing lamps, weary mind,
> Past the town, Cold Mountain Temple
> Midnight bells the traveller's skiff

The collection also displayed a document in Chinese and Syriac about a Nestorian Christian church established there in 631AD. Kircher devotes much of his book to it. Islam came later – and has stayed. But in that year of 631, a monk was heading west out of the T'ang dominions, along the Silk Road and round to the Ganges. In 645 he brought back the Buddhist scriptures, and the Little Wild Goose Pagoda – still standing – was built for their protection and study. His journey became the stuff of legends, which were set down in the Ming dynasty as 'The Journey to the West', of which 'Monkey' is an episode. I'd just got round to reading it.

Bibliography

Ch'eng-ên, Wu, *Monkey*, translated by Arthur Waley, London, 1942,
    3rd impression 1943

Bouvier, Nicolas, *l'Usage du monde*, Droz, 1963; reissued by Payot, 1992

Eitel, Ernest, J., *Handbook of Chinese Buddhism*, second edition, HongKong, 1888

Overy, Richard, *Russia's War*, Allen Lane/Penguin, Harmondsworth, 1998

Malcolm Caldwell's South-East Asia, South-East Asian monograph series No. 5,
    James Cook University, Queensland, 1979

Richards, Hamish & Richards, Geraint J., *Effective Corporate Sector Strategies
    Aimed at Alleviating the Plight of Street Children*, Lakeside Publishing,
    Cardiff, 1996

*La Chine d'Athanase Kirchere de la Compagnie de Jésus, illustré de plusieurs
    monuments tant sacrés que profanes,* translated by F. S. Dalquié, reprinted
    Geneva, 1980

Wai-Lim Yip, ed. and trans., *Chinese Poetry: An Anthology of Modes and Genres*,
    Duke University Press, Durham and London, 1997

Shestov, Lev, *In Job's Balances*, translated by Camilla Coventry,
    Ohio University Press, Athens, 1975

Fondane, Benjamin, *Rencontres avec Léon Chestov*, Plasma, Paris, 1982

Kuppner, Frank, *A Bad Day for the Sung Dynasty*, Carcanet, Manchester, 1985

Heinzmann, Uni-solar, Trek

Simon Starling

Heinzmann, Uni-solar, Trek.
Unité d'Habitation de Briey-en-Forêt to Unité d'Habitation de Rezé.

2273 grams of reading matter for a five day journey from Unité d'Habitation de Briey-en-Forêt (Le Corbusier, 1957) to Unité d'Habitation de Rezé (Le Corbusier, 1955) on a Trek 7300 bicycle powered by a Heinzmann 200 watt electric motor, recharged daily with three Uni-solar 32watt flexible solar panels, 23rd–27th August, 2000.

France, Carte Routière et Touristique, Michelin (No.989)	
1/1000 000 – 1cm : 10km	49gm
Uni-solar Battery Charger Manual, Triple Junction Technology	63gm
Bicycle Owner's Manual, Trek Bicycle Corporation	182gm
Heinzmann Electric Bicycles, Part A: Operating Instructions,	
Fritz Heinzmann, GmbH&Co	122gm
The Le Corbusier Guide, Deborah Gans, Princeton	
Architectural Press	501gm
Flesh and Stone: The Body and the City in Western Civilization,	
Richard Sennett, Faber & Faber	682gm
Lightness: The Inevitable Renaissance of Minimum Energy	
Structures, Adriaan Beukers & Ed van Hinte, 010	468gm
The Girls' Guide to Hunting & Fishing, Melissa Banks, Penguin	206gm

Total 2273gm

Excess Baggage

Solar Living Source Book: The Complete Guide to Renewable	
Energy Technologies & Sustainable Living, John Schaeffer,	
Real Goods,(Printed with soya based inks on 100%	
recycled paper)	1554gm
Your Private Sky: R. Buckminster Fuller, The Art of Design Science,	
J. Krausse (ed.), Claude Lichtenstein, Lars Müller	1399gm

Le Corbusier and The Tragic View of Architecture, Charles Jencks,
    Penguin   508gm
Energies: An Illustrated Guide to the Biosphere and Civilisation,
    Vaclav Smil, MIT Press   689gm
Bas Jan Ader, Brad Spence & Thomas Crow, The Art Gallery,
    University of California, Irvine   315gm
The Third Policeman, Flann O'Brien,
    Flamingo Modern Classics   164gm

Navigating the geography of modern society requires very little physical effort, hence engagement; indeed, as roads become straightened and regularised, the voyager need account less and less for the people and the buildings on the street in order to move, making minute motions in an ever less complex environment. The traveller, like the television viewer, experiences the world in narcotic terms; the body moves passively to destinations set in a fragmented and discontinuous urban geography.

Richard Sennett, *Flesh and Stone*

"You don't use a computer?" I say, which seems like the most mundane question I could ask.
    "Just for the animation" he says. "I'm a Luddite like you, on your – " he whispers, "Quiet Deluxe."
    I don't know what a Luddite is, but Bonnie won't let me ask.

Melissa Banks, *The Girl's Guide to Hunting and Fishing*

Simon Starling

A Utopian Bookshelf

Ross Birrell

Bibliography

Arblaster, Anthony, & Lukes, Steven, (eds.), *The Good Society: A Book of Readings*, Methuen, London, 1971

Beecher & Bienvenu, *The Utopian Vision of Charles Fourier*, Jonathan Cape, London, 1972

Bloch, Ernst, *The Principle of Hope*, Volumes 1-3, MIT Press, Cambridge, Mass., 1998

Buck-Morss, Susan, Stallabrass, Julian, Donskis, Leonidas, (eds.), *Ground Control: Technology and Utopia*, Black Dog, London, 1997

Buckminster Fuller, R., *Utopia or Oblivion: The Prospect for Humanity*, Penguin, Harmondsworth, 1969

Carey, John (ed.), *The Faber Book of Utopias,* Faber, London, 1999

Claeys, Gregory, & Tower Sargent, Lyman, (eds.), *The Utopia Reader*, New York University Press, New York, 1999

Davis, James C., *Utopia and the Ideal Society*, Cambridge University Press, Cambridge, 1981

Erasmus, Charles J., *In Search of the Common Good: Utopian Experiments Past and Future*, Free Press, New York, 1977

Goodman, Paul, *Utopian Essays and Practical Proposals*, Vintage, New York, 1964

Harvey, David, *Spaces of Hope*, Edinburgh University Press, 2000

Haworth, Lawrence, *The Good City*, Indiana University Press, Bloomington, 1966

Home, Stewart, *The Assault on Culture: Utopian Currents from Lettrisme to Class War*, AK Press, Stirling, 1991

Kumar, Krishan, *Utopianism*, Open University Press, Milton Keynes 1991

Manuel, Frank, & Manuel, Fritzie, *Utopian Thought in the Western World*, Blackwell, Oxford, 1979

More, Thomas, *Utopia*, Everyman, London, 1985

Nozick, Robert, *Anarchy, State, and Utopia*, Blackwell, Oxford, 1974

Owen, Robert, *A New Vision of Society and Other Writings*, Penguin, Harmondsworth, 1991

Paine, Thomas, *The Rights of Man*, Penguin, Harmondsworth, 1976

Panitch, Leo, & Leys, Colin, (eds.), *Necessary and Unnecessary Utopias*, Socialist Register 2000, Merlin Press, Suffolk, 1999

Plato, *The Republic*, Everyman, London, 1935

Sade, D.A.F. de, *120 Days of Sodom & Other Writings*, Grove Press, New York, 1966

Sargisson, Lucy, *Contemporary Feminist Utopianism*, Routledge, London, 1996

Schaer, Claeys, Sargent, *Utopia: The Search for the Ideal Society in the Western World*, New York Public Library/Oxford, 2000

Stansill, P., & Zane Mairowitz, D., *Bamn: Outlaw Manifestos and Ephemera 1965-1970*, Penguin, Harmondsworth, 1971

Tafuri, Manfredo, *Architecture and Utopia: Design and Capitalist Development*, MIT Press, Cambridge, Mass. 1976

Thoreau, Henry David, *Walden and Civil Disobedience*, Penguin, Harmondsworth, 1987

Trocchi, Alexander, *The Invisible Insurrection of a Million Minds: A Trocchi Reader*, edited by Andrew Murray Scott, Polygon, Edinburgh, 1991

Vaneigem, Raoul, *The Revolution of Everyday Life*, Left Bank Books & Rebel Press, London, 1983

Wallerstein, Immanuel, *Utopistics or, Historical Choices for the Twenty-first Century*, New Press, New York, 1988

Ward, Colin, *Utopia*, Penguin Education, Harmondsworth, 1974

Ross Birrell

Unrevealed Religion

Kevin Henderson

Unrevealed Religion

Marcus Aurelius' *Meditations*, a 'commonplace book', reveals a mind of imposing humility formed in the Stoic tradition, to whom philosophy meant everything that a religion can mean – *Meditations* is a 'manual' for living, a journal of personal devotion.

Bittersweet Within My Heart records the passing thoughts of Mary Queen of Scots on life, death, love, politics and faith. Her final Sonnet, written at Fotheringhay Castle on the eve of her execution, concludes

> There is nothing worthwhile I can do;
> Ask only that my misery should cease
> And that, being punished in a world like this, I have my portion in
>   eternal bliss.

Mary's desire to earn her reward in heaven is tempered here (on earth) by the knowledge she can do no more before taking up what she believes awaits her 'on the other side' – stoic, tranquil, the Scottish Queen accepts her fate: 'I have my portion in eternal bliss'. The last line of *Meditations* reads: 'Pass on your way, then, with a smiling face, under the smile of him who bids you go'.

Wilfred Owen's 'Anthem For Doomed Youth' was written at Craiglockhart Hospital in the Autumn of 1917 and opens, bitterly, with the question: 'What passing-bells for these who die as cattle?' He laments the fact that those slaughtered by 'The shrill, demented choirs of wailing shells . . .' will not receive a Christian funeral but a brutal parody of one: the 'bugles calling for them from sad shires' once called them to 'the front' but now sound the 'Last Post'. In the closing lines we begin to see Owen's idea of devotion as trauma:

> The pallor of girls' brows shall be their pall;
> Their flowers the tenderness of patient minds,
> And each slow dusk a drawing-down of blinds.

In, *The Great War and Modern Memory*, Paul Fussell notes that sunrise and sunset feature prominently in the literature of the Great War. These were times 'of heightened ritual anxiety' – a cruel reversal of over one hundred years of Romantic poetry (and painting) where they once represented peace, hope and pastoral charm.

Louise Glück's collection *The Wild Iris* is a *lieder* cycle written in the 'language of flowers (the Biblical lilies of the field)'; the language of Spring and natural resurrection, sunrise and sunset. Glück questions (searches for) the place of devotional faith (of 'unrevealed religion'). Many of the poems address the silent figure of God. In 'Sunset' she writes:

> You have no faith in your own language.
> So you invest
> authority in signs
> you cannot read with any accuracy.

To create an ironic moment, it was enough for a soldier-poet during the Great War to compare a sunset or sunrise (God's work) to the blood-drenched land (man's work) he looked upon each stand-to. That spring was the best time of year for offensives adds further irony, prompting T. S. Eliot, four years after the war, to write : 'April is the cruellest month, breeding / Lilacs out of the dead land ... '. Glück reclaims this 'authority of signs' for a Romantic ('confessional') tradition – one now characterised by troubled and uncertain political and socio-religious reflection. Her fields invoke 'The Flowers of the Forest'; they are both 'Waste Land' and 'Garden of Eden'.

Kevin Henderson

Bibliography

Aurelius, Marcus, *Meditations*, Maxwell Staniforth (trans.), Penguin Books, 1977

Bittersweet Within My Heart: The Collected Poems of Mary Queen of Scots,
    Robin Bell. (trans. & ed.), Pavilion Books Ltd., 1995

Owen, Wilfred, *The War Poems*, Jon Stallworthy (ed.), Chatto & Windus Ltd., 1994

Fussell, Paul, *The Great War and Modern Memory*, Oxford University Press, 2000

Glück, Louise, *The Wild Iris*, The Ecco Press, 1993

Eliot, T. S., *The Complete Poems and Plays of T.S. Eliot*, Faber & Faber, 1982

Scots Guards Standard Settings of Pipe Music Volume 1:240-241

'Where Music Enters'
Norma Cole

85

La fleur inverse

THE EVIDENCE OF THINGS NOT SEEN — JAMES BALDWIN

DISCREPANT ENGAGEMENT

ROBERT FINCH

UNIVERSITY OF TORONTO PRESS

Alabama

THE SIXTH SENSE

PILLING: Beckett before Godot

Collected Poems in English and French: Samuel Beckett

CAMBRIDGE

The Embodied Mind
Varela, Thompson, and Rosch

VAIL / WHITE
Power and the Praise Poem
Southern African Voices in History

PRESENT
ROBIN

'Where Music Enters'

The order of the books is peculiar (particular). That is, they are not listed in alphabetical order. I didn't find them in alphabetical order, nor do I keep them that way (see photo).

They move.

There are three books listed that are not in the photograph. I gave one away and reordered it but it has not yet arrived, the others are currently not to hand. But they are no less present. There is, too, the implied presence of all the books of poetry, and all the other books ...

Morris, Robert, *From Mnemosyne to Clio: The Mirror to the Labyrinth (1998-1999-2000)*, Musée d'Art contemporain, Lyon, 2000; Skira, Milan, 2000

> *Some works might be looked at as strategies for forgetting. Some of the so-called 'Anti-Form' pieces of 1967-1969 were capable of an indeterminate set of formal 'moments' without any final configuration; they worked to 'forget' their form.*
>
> Morris, p247

Feraoun, Mouloud, *Journal 1955-1962: Reflections on the French-Algerian War*, edited and with an introduction by James D. Le Sueur, translated by Mary Ellen Wolf and Claude Fouillade, University of Nebraska Press, Lincoln and London, 2000

> *The olive plantations are scorched, and the olive trees are burning like torches, along with the fig trees and other fruit-bearing trees. What happened is exactly what happened centuries ago when the Vandals came and set fire to the Roman plantations. This proves that the face of war is always the same ...*
>
> Feraoun, p219

Pesic, Peter, *Labyrinth: A Search for the Hidden Meaning of Science,* The MIT Press, Cambridge, Massachusetts and London, England, 2000

> ... *the nature of things betrays itself more readily under the vexations of art than in its natural freedom.*
>
> Francis Bacon, Pesic, p21

Roubaud, Jacques, *La fleur inverse: Essai sur l'art formel des troubadours,* Editions Ramsay, Paris, 1986

> *et er la tenzos de non re*
>
> Aimeric de Peguilhan, in Roubaud, p23

Kravitt, Edward F., *The Lied: Mirror of Late Romanticism,* Yale University Press, New Haven and London, 1996

> *The atonal network of* Hanging Gardens *is, indeed, equivocal. Further, Schoenberg's interweaving of asymmetric melodic structure and flexible rhythm within the atonal network creates an ambiguity no earlier composer had achieved.*
>
> Kravitt, p158

Byrd, Don, *The Poetics of the Common Knowledge,* State University of New York Press, Albany, 1994

> *The world is becoming invisible.*
>
> Rilke, in Byrd, p263

Attali, Jacques, *Noise: The Political Economy of Music,* translated by Brian Massumi, Foreword by Frederic Jameson, Afterword by Susan McClary, University of Minneapolis Press, Minneapolis/London, 1985

> *Composition liberates time so that it can be lived, not stockpiled.*
>
> Attali, p145

Brand, Stewart, *The Clock of the Long Now: Time and Responsibility: The Ideas Behind the World's Slowest Computer,* Basic Books, New York, 1999

> *Time is a ride and you are on it.*
>
> Daniel Hillis in Brand, p69

Gullan-Whur, Margaret, *Within Reason: A Life of Spinoza*, St. Martin's Press, New York, 1998

> *... he held that the mind was the idea of the body ...*
>
> Gullan-Whur, xiii

Spencer, Jon Michael, *The Rhythms of Black Folk: Race, Religion and Pan-Africanism*, Africa World Press, Trenton NJ, 1995

> *It too requires a certain rhythm – 'off-timing' – which is a part of our culture of rhythmic confidence.*
>
> Spencer, p141

Hazard, Mary E., *Elizabethan Silent Language*, University of Nebraska Press, Lincoln and London, 2000

> *The typographical shapes render visible a spatial configuration of thought.*
>
> Hazard, p57

Bargebuhr, Frederick P., *The Alhambra: A Cycle of Studies on the Eleventh Century in Moorish Spain*, Walter de Gruyter & Co., Berlin, 1968

> *Excursus: Full Moon or Sickle Moon?*
>
> Bargebuhr, p287

Barker, Francis, *The Tremulous Private Body: Essays on Subjection*, Methuen, London and New York, 1984

> *If Hamlet called on discourse to hold a mirror up to nature, at least the mirror could be seen for what it was.*
>
> Barker, p18

Baldwin, James, *The Evidence of Things Not Seen*, Foreword by Derrick Bell with Janet Dewart Bell, Henry Holt & Co., New York, 1985, 1995

> *Bring out your dead.*
>
> Baldwin, p39

Mackey, Nathaniel, *Discrepant Engagement: Dissonance, Cross-Culturality, and Experimental Writing*, The University of Alabama Press, Tuscaloosa, 1993

Though Williams and Miller insist that Bunk Johnson doesn't stammer, the limp he inflicts on the melody is ancestral to the stutter of Monk, Rollins, and others.

Mackey, p252

Finch, Robert, *The Sixth Sense: Individualism in French Poetry 1686-1760*, University of Toronto Press, Toronto, 1966

It is unlikely that the bisecting into 'literature' and 'thought' will much longer continue to find favour in those academic circles where it still persists.

Finch, p304

Alighieri, Dante, *La Vita Nuova (The New Life)*, translated and illustrated by Dante Gabriel Rossetti, with the Fifth Canto of Dante's *Inferno* and Rossetti's two illustrations thereto, George Routledge & Sons Ltd, London, E. P. Dutton & Co., New York, nd

With this speech he was away, and my sleep was broken up.

Dante, p27

McGann, Jerome, *Dante Gabriel Rossetti and the Game That Must Be Lost*, Yale University Press, New Haven & London, 2000

The most literal house of Rossetti's life, his famous lodgings near the river at 16 Cheyne Walk, emblemizes the machinery of his mind. In its six rooms were no fewer than thirty-four mirrors – ten in the dining room alone.

McGann, p26

Beckett, Samuel, *Collected Poems in French and English*, Grove Press, Inc., New York, 1977

> *A woman every night*
> *Journeys secretly.*

Paul Eluard, 'L'univers-solitude' Beckett's translation, Beckett, p79

Pilling, John, *Beckett Before Godot*, Cambridge University Press, Cambridge, United Kingdom, 1997

> *There are times, above all in Europe, when the road reflects better than the mirror.*

Beckett in Pilling, p167

Varela, Francisco J., *Ethical Know-How: Action, Wisdom, and Cognition*, Stanford University Press, Stanford, California, 1999

> *Like a jam session, the environment inspires the neural 'music' of the cognitive system.*

Varela, p56

Varela Francisco J., Thompson, Evan, & Rosch, Elizabeth, *The Embodied Mind: Cognitive Science and Human Experience*, The MIT Press, Cambridge, Massachusetts and London, England, 1991

> *What is remarkable about this passage is the absence of any notion of representation.*

Varela et al, 139

Vail, Leroy & White, Landeg, *Power and the Praise Poem: Southern African Voices in History*, University Press of Virginia, Charlottesville, and James Currey, London, 1991

> *Paiva, I have killed his money*
> *for him.*
> *His penis!*

Plantation workers' song, Mozambique, in Vail & Landeg, p199

Lewinter, Roger, *Stéphane Mallarmé: La Musique et les lettres, Crise de vers,* Lecture des textes (CD): Roger Lewinter, Éditions Ivréa, Paris, 1999

Orage, lustral; et dans des bouleversements, tout à l'aquit de la génération récente, l'acte d'écrire se scruta jusqu'en origine.

Lewinter, p11

Fikentscher, Kai, *'You Better Work!': Underground Dance Music in New York City,* Wesleyan University Press, Hanover & London, 2000

The song does not remain the same.

Fikentscher, 47

Ueno, Osamu, 'Res nobis similis: Desire and the Double in Spinoza', in *Desire and Affect: Spinoza as Psychologist,* Yirmiyahu Yovel (ed.), Little Room Press, New York, 1999

Desire is therefore the desire to imagine.

Ueno, p83

Abraham, Nicolas, *RHYTHMS: On the Work, Translation, and Psychoanalysis,* translated by Benjamin Thigpen and Nicholas T. Rand, Stanford University Press, Stanford, California, 1995

To abandon oneself to a rhythm is momentarily to cease positing the existence of the surrounding world.

Abraham, p21

Merleau-Ponty, Maurice, *L'Oeil et L'Esprit.* Gallimard, Paris, 1964

Si les créations ne sont pas un acquis, ce n'est pas seulement que, comme toutes choses, elles passent, c'est aussi qu'elles ont presque toute leur vie devant elles.

Merleau-Ponty, p92-3

The Books of Song
Brian Catling

The books of song have been

The books of prayer have been

The books of parable have been

The books of divinity have been

& the books of hope have been

bleached away by the rain

starved out by the sun

eaten away by frost

rubbed out by snow

cleansed by the persistent wind

The Libraries of Thought & Imagination

Previous page: 'Twelve Who Ruled' (O. M. Ungers Private Library)
Ian Hamilton Finlay, 1990; photograph by Werner J. Hannappel

A Caravan Collection

Gerry Cambridge

A Caravan Collection

For the first thirty-seven of my forty-two years, with occasional exceptions of a month or two, I lived in a caravan. The last twenty of those years I spent in the same caravan on a small site in rural Ayrshire. It had two main advantages. The rent, just £14 a week when I finally left, was cheap. And the site was surrounded by countryside. The caravan had no running water, a result of a winter leak, which rotted half the chipboard floor and left me, Sir Impractical, paranoid about burst pipes. Though it was plumbed in, I took fourteen years to connect up the pipes again. I recall a character in a Gavin Maxwell book asking the whereabouts of the toilet. "Why," came the reply, "the whole hillside is a toilet!" I had a toilet block two hundred yards distant, but the adjacent hedge also served in moments of desperation. And the lack of running water was a good excuse to learn the constellations. There was little else to look at, while filling a bucket with water at an outside tap on a starry night.

When I left it in 1997, to become Writer-in-Residence at Hugh MacDiarmid's cottage, Brownsbank, I had lived on the caravan site at least a decade longer than my nearest rival in endurance. 'Endurance' is, perhaps, an exaggeration. I often enjoyed living so near the ground that if I fell over, speaking metaphorically, I hardly knew about it. I liked to open the kitchen door on a winter night to the Universe, infinite beyond my small lit cell: the Pleiades setting in the West, the Plough glinting over the witch-wood. I sometimes enjoyed being aware of the rain drumming on the roof, even as I knew it would worsen the leak in the corner of the bedroom, which grew steadily more extensive during my residence. It had been a mere drip at first. My attempt to fix it brought only a slow spreading seepage that buckled half the ceiling in the bedroom. I have always distrusted the physical universe.

The caravan. Twenty-eight feet by nine feet of aluminium, chipboard, and iron. I bought it secondhand, or 'previously-enjoyed', as I have heard it termed, for £600 in 1977. I was eighteen, and temporarily solvent. The caravan. A fridge in winter. An oven (turned on) in summer. On frosty nights, caravans produce condensation. The windows literally weep with it. This then freezes when the occupants go to bed, and forms a spectacular coating of ice ferns brash across the windows by morning. In the blue light of dawn, it looks as if the windows have all developed cataracts.

"And did you have books in this caravan?" a friend once asked. Yes, I had books. I had so many books they probably prevented the structure being scattered across Ayrshire in the winter gales. I had so many that, shortly before I had to have the caravan scrapped, I didn't just select my chosen book from a shelf, unless I was lucky. I had to go on an expedition to find my book. I had to excavate my book, aided by a vague memory of its being somewhere behind the fifth stack in the corner, stacks so perilously balanced that one wrong move would send them toppling, like dominoes. By the end, I didn't 'have' a library. I lived in one. Actually, 'library' is an over-glamorous description. I lived in a dusty, chaotic, caravan warehouse of books, a cornucopia messy and shambling as the internet. I took to worrying that the main bookcase would fall forward and kill my cat as she slept on the couch below, a worry allayed by attaching the bookcase by a metal bracket to a wooden partition dividing the living room from the kitchen. The shelves were so buckled and bowed by volumes that were their wood a sound it would have been a shriek.

In line with my policy of basic living, I possessed no TV. Quizzed on this by the licensing people, I wrote, with the pomposity of the twenty-year-old caravan intellectual, that I preferred reading Wittgenstein's *Tractacus*, a book I had only recently heard of and thought sounded impressive. A dilatory autodidact, I have always aspired to scholarship.

My unofficial career as book collector and reader had begun, albeit with comics, long before I owned the caravan. When I was nine, living in Hampshire with my family, every Saturday morning I would cycle the mile into the village of Fawley to pick up my Marvel comic at the newsagents. *Captain America! Spider Man! Thor the Thunder God! The X-Men* (and one token woman)! I was so taken with Thor and his continual battles with Loki, god of the underworld, that I had one of my uncles make me a mallet like Thor's, but from wood. The real Thor was the only person who could lift his mallet. The real Thor's mallet, when he threw it at something (which he did only at the bad guys such as Loki) always returned to him, like a boomerang.

My mallet refused to obey similar laws. It could be lifted by anyone, even my younger sister. It never returned to me of its own accord. I had to go and get it. Further, unlike Thor's, it never sped clean as an arrow to its target, but twirled over and over, chaotically, like a catherine wheel: an early lesson on the distance between fantasy and reality. I also recall another character, Namor the Submariner, 'Lord of Atlantis', of stunning physique, and amphibious. He had little wings on his ankles and webs between his fingers. He was equally at home in the upper air or in the cold gloomy reaches of the sea. Then there was Dr Strange, haunter of the gusty urban alleys, with his 'amulet': the first time I had encountered the word. When the TV flickered or misbehaved, I would narrow my eyes and concentrate on making it return to normal. That's what Dr. Strange would have done.

One day when I was eleven or twelve, at Birtley in country Durham, I was introduced to bird-nesting by the local boys. Egg-collecting became a temporary passion. The first real book I spent my 'own' money on cost 50p. It was the little Observer's *Book of British Birds*, published by Frederick Warne, printed on glossy paper in a pocket format, complete with colour and black and white plates by Archibald Thorburn. I remember looking through it and being fascinated that all these creatures existed, out there around me, in the world.

Which didn't stop me stealing their eggs. But by the time I was fourteen I had graduated to morality, where birds were concerned. My second major book was the AA *Book of British Birds*. It so enamoured me as a bird-obsessed fifteen year old that I wrote about it for my English 'O' level. Its Latin names were a litany I would recite silently to myself in the face of threatening females. My first book, then, was a key. My second book, let me face it, was a woman-substitute.

The books we buy, whether from Oxfam or Thins, are an external guide to our admissable inner weathers. In my early twenties, I took to photographing moths, or crabs in aquaria, or dragonflies in little sets on my kitchen table; I bought photographic books. When I was twenty-four, writing hack journalism for *Reader's Digest* and others, I began writing poetry. My shelves filled slowly with anthologies and volumes by individual poets. By 1997, these included the two limited editions of A. D. Hope, the Australian poet, sent me by his son after I wrote to the old poet, now bedridden, requesting a poem for my poetry magazine, *The Dark Horse*. They included books like the Penguin *Selected Poems* of Robert Frost, edited by Ian Hamilton, which I bought in Kilmarnock. I read it so often that the pages were falling out.

Books can also have a talismanic quality. I recall finding Edwin Morgan's signed copy of the American poet X. J. Kennedy's *An Introduction to Poetry* in Voltaire and Rousseau's in Glasgow, years before I met either poet. One summer day, after being dragged out of a pub where England were playing Scotland, I discovered in a Shelter shop in the Byres Road a slim, undistinguished looking hardback called *Cage Without Grievance*, published in Glasgow in 1942. The author was

W. S. Graham. The book is signed and dated by the poet in a beautiful, cursive, flamboyant script, using a fountain pen with a flexible nib (not to be found in modern pens) and inscribed to Norman Thompson. The introduction to Graham's *The Nightfisherman: Selected Letters*, adds an interesting detail: it was Norman Thompson who introduced Graham to Edwin Morgan, which led to an important friendship for both poets. I was recently informed by Michael Snow, co-editor of the letters, that my copy of *Cage Without Grievance* is probably worth at least £200. It cost me 50p. I am not tempted to sell it. Although he only did so for three or four years, Graham lived in a caravan too.

I have a confession to make. I am trying to cure myself of my propensity for book collecting. When I left for Brownsbank, my library, that is, my caravan, had to be scrapped. Up into my parents' loft most of my books went, in boxes and suitcases and black bags.

So many books went up there that, for a while, I worried about the safety of my parents sleeping in the bedroom below. I imagined them buried under a small mountain as they lay in their bed, only their feet left sticking out, giving new meaning to the phrase, 'lost in books'.

Someday, I am confident, I will retrieve them all. I think of them there in the darkness, packed in boxes, title on title, silent and rather mysterious, their purchase a record of forgotten days in Voltaire and Rousseau's, or numerous Oxfams.

The book is dead? Long live the book, say I. Long live my parents, too.

Gerry Cambridge

An Encounter

Tom Leonard

An Encounter

The place where a democratic freedom of encounter with Literature has occurred is in the free public libraries. It is not that they haven't operated censorship, but the public libraries have remained the one place where anyone can build his or her relation with the literary world. It was in the public library in Pollok that I built mine. The '5–7' department, just a green tin cupboard with about eight shelves, and the books facing out the way. You had to wrap your books in newspaper and you had to show your hands. Then the day when I could use the Junior Department for the '7-14s', a whole wall under the window. Real books at last, that wouldn't be finished the moment you got home. Of course the time came when the junior department wasn't what I wanted, but I wasn't old enough yet for the adult. I got to know the names of the authors in the A to C section of the adult section that adjoined the Junior wall at the far end. The adult fiction went right round two walls of the building, with non-fiction in standing shelves between. What a day that would be, when you could get into that. My mother let me take the bus to Govan to use the Junior Department at Elder Park. It seemed enormous, as big as Pollock's adult section; it had a very quiet atmosphere I'll never forget, with really heavy stone walls, and the pillars you went in at the entrance. It was there I got to know Dickens. Then the adult section at Pollok. Then the Stirling, the Mecca of them all.

The public libraries gave me the education I wanted. Like most Scottish writers I know of my generation, I went to school and got British – mainly English – Literature. I went to the library and borrowed American, Russian and European. And these were the ones that mattered as far as I was concerned. When the hero of *Crime and Punishment* ran down the stairs of a close after the murder, I knew what it was he ran down. All the poetry that meant anything to me in my middle teens, when I first got to like poetry – all of it that meant anything to me, I got out the library. You could choose what you wanted there, read it in your own house, say exactly what you wanted about it, or - most precious right of all - you could say absolutely nothing about it whatever.

In my early twenties I worked in a university bookshop. I hated it. You might as well be selling bananas, and the pay was rubbish. A non-union place, I was young, and it took the work inspectorate to call and pin up the minimum workshop rates for me to find out I was being paid less than the legal minimum for shopworkers. I decided to try to get to university, and studied at night to make up my Highers. At dinner time I would sometimes make it to the library at St George's Cross, and get a quick half hour in the reading room. Other times in the Mitchell Library at Charing Cross, not getting on with my Highers but sitting with a book called *The Annotated Index to the Cantos of Ezra Pound*, writing in pencil in the margin of my own copy of Pound's poems, the references from the index. This was my education.

I did get in to university, and at the second attempt got the degree in English and Scottish Literature that gave me the bit of paper that now matters to me. That paper I renew every year for £5: the membership card to Glasgow University Library. That Library is specialised, and offers a specialised view of the world. Its filters have excluded literature by working-class people, though there are books in plenty about 'them'. You have to go elsewhere for original literature itself.

In some ways it's here that the public libraries come into their own, and in other ways it is where they have been most frustrating. The public libraries have been where millions including myself have received their education beyond basic literacy that actually mattered to them; but while the public have been out front borrowing books, through the back there has always been the world you see over the librarian's shoulder when they go to the phone, those rooms with half-opened doors marked Private that they put the light on when they go through. Always when I have requested a book at the Mitchell Reference Library in Glasgow, and when someone has later appeared to hand the book over at the counter, there has always been that pleasant smile between us as if isn't it lucky a wee fairy turned up with the right book just out of sight round the corner. And always I've thought at the back of my mind, I wonder what it looks like where you've been.

Tom Leonard
from the Introduction to *Radical Renfrew*

The Burning of the Books
Edwin Morgan

The Burning of the Books

from 'From the Video Box'

I

I saw that Burning of the Books, in China
I don't know how many centuries B.C.
If anything was compulsive on the set,
that was. You could almost feel the heat,
and when you saw the soldiers and flunkeys dancing
like demons against the glare, bending and lifting,
lifting and throwing, throwing and grimacing through the sparks,
and when you heard the crackle and spit of the wood
going off like fireworks, and they had fireworks too,
or I think they had, it was hard to be sure,
but anyway the bonfires getting bigger and bigger
and those gongs looming and booming in the smoke,
when you'd seen and heard all that,
I thought it was the best the old classics
had ever done for them, to warm a few hands
in a freezing night like that: there were no long faces,
I noticed, and no one ran with tongs
to snatch a few analects out of the flames.
This was first-class entertainment.
That emperor has the right idea.
That's really all I wanted to say.

II

I have just watched that fearful programmme
of the burning of the Library at Alexandria.
I rushed to the box – I am still shaking –
to record my disgust that any producer
should foist such barbarous philistinism –
without introduction, without discussion –
on a million homes. Accident, arson, act of war –
I don't care what the miserable excuse is
for showing the death of books, live, on screen.
Men, I could understand; but books! –
all right, call them rolls, scrolls, codexes –
not one, not ten, oh no, but tens of thousands,
irreplaceable, perishable, unprinted, unique!
That was the grandeur that was Rome did that.
Then they had the nerve to show us an epilogue
when anything that was left six centuries later
was burned by the Arabs as pagan trash.
I shall certainly write straight to the Authority.
There are limits to what an ordinary man
can stomach, or should stomach. I admit my wife
was not worried, but then not everyone is a reader;
I'm sure she supports me though. Well I think that's it.

Edwin Morgan

115

A Relationship Between Books (1994)
Douglas Gordon

A Relationship Between Books
Proposal for the Attention of Bernhard Starkmann.

November 30th, 1993

Dear Bernhard,

It has been some time now since we met in XXXX Street to discuss the possibility of making a specific work for you. I have spent a long time thinking through how to realise this 'relationship' (as this is how I see it).

The basis for my proposal might be said to be rooted in certain ideas of genuine and constructed coincidence. I like the fact that your 'work' is in books and this allows you to collect art, whereas my 'work' is art and this allows me to collect books. This is the genuine coincidence.

The constructed coincidence is the proposed work, the title of which is 'A Relationship Between Books (and other published material)'.

My idea is for us to establish this relationship by initiating 'twin' libraries; the contents of which will be defined by me. By this I mean that there will exist two collections of publications; identical but separate. The practical application of this idea is that where I would normally buy one copy of a book I will now buy two and send the other copy to the 'twin' collection. This process will be initiated on completion and receipt of a full contract, the first part of which you are reading now.

The full contract will explain, in detail, the terms of a relationship where I undertake to send you a copy of every book or published piece that I purchase from the time of the agreement.

Each book (yours and mine) will be stamped to indicate (1) the time of purchase (2) the place of purchase (3) the price of purchase (4) the authenticity of the object in relation to the project i.e. the publication will be signed and numbered by me.

The financial maintenance of the project will be borne by the owner of the work. The complete contract will detail an arrangement where the artist will receive an initial fee and thereafter will be 'reimbursed' for the cost price of each subsequent object sent to the 'twin' library.

The arrangement and display of the library is an issue which I have chosen not to deal with. The priority for this work is in the process of collecting, cataloguing and sending the material. I see the diligent administration of this work to be more important than the formal considerations of a public or private display. In other words, the library may be shown at the discretion of the owner, and by a means which he seeks to complement the idea. Also, a list of the collected works may be published or exhibited at the discretion of the owner.

As you can see, this is a project which demands some degree of trust between individuals; an issue for artists and collectors. It also addresses the role of information in our culture, and specifically sets out to demystify the aura of the artist by revealing a significant amount of personal taste, prejudice and influence.

In regards to the 'time factor', it is my intention that the project will be ongoing from the time of the completed contract until termination, if indeed that is necessary. It is also my intention that the project need only be terminated on the express wishes of the owner, or the expiry of one or both individuals involved. Once more, the full contract will make this clearer.

I look forward to hearing your views on this proposal, and I hope it communicates the challenge that I intend in the event that we activate the project.

Douglas Gordon

17 BULSTRODE STREET
LONDON W1M 5FQ
0171-935 5372

14 March 1995

Dear Douglas,

1. In January 1994, you proposed to me a unique artistic work ('the Work') to be initiated in the spirit of the attached essay by Walter Benjamin entitled 'Book Collecting' which would be created by you, an artist who buys books and me, a professional seller of books who buys art. The work is to be entitled 'A Relationship Between Books 1994 –' ('the Title').

As a consequence of my one-time payment to you of £2,000 the Work has been and will be developed exclusively by us as joint owners of all rights (including applicable copyrights in any related printed, video, audio, etc materials) during the period 1 January 1994 through 31 December 1997 ('the Collection Period') on the following basis:

a. During the Collection Period, each time you purchase a book for yourself, you shall purchase an additional copy for me and if such additional copy is unavailable then you shall not purchase your own copy. Promptly following your purchase of both copies, you shall write in each copy the date purchased, the purchase location and the price, you shall keep a purchase receipt when practicable and you shall send my copy to me by post. Accordingly, we each shall be maintaining a 'twin' library consisting of these purchased books which initially shall be kept geographically apart but be connected by the selection and distribution concept and process and ultimately by its combined eventual permanent public display by an Approved Recipient (as defined below) (individually 'Twin Library' and together, 'The Twin Libraries').

b. You shall pay for the copy of each book purchased by you for your twin Library from your own financial resources and, unless already paid for by me, each copy purchased for my Twin Library and the cost of its delivery to me will be paid for from the £3,200 which has been advanced to you by me for such purpose ('the Fund'). At such time during the Collection Period the total amount of the Fund has been disbursed, or you have died, then unless otherwise agreed to by us, the Twin Libraries will be deemed to be complete and, for future reference purposes, the year in which such events occurs shall be added to the end of the Title.

c. Without each others prior written consent, no book in either Twin Library can be sold or otherwise disposed of. Once it has been mutually agreed that a book can be sold, then 'its twin' must also be sold and the proceeds from both sales shall be used by you to acquire a replacement book for each Twin Library on the basis set out herein.

d. During the Collection Period and until such time as the Twin Libraries have been eventually permanently displayed by an Approved Recipient, neither of us will be under any obligation to display the contents of his Twin Library but each of us shall take all reasonable steps to maintain its safety and integrity (although insurance will not be required) and to ensure that both of us are kept aware from time to time of the actual location of its contents. In this connection, each of us will send to the other at least every 12 months a photograph of the state in which his Twin Library is maintained at that time which, amongst other related materials, will be an integral part of the Work.

Bernhard Starkmann

Meeting #7

The Murder Mystery Section (under M) of any Public Library in Great Britain just before closing time on March 24th, 2006.

Reading Burns to the
Scott Monument, Edinburgh, 1999

Nathan Coley

Visions of the Western Railways

Alan Halsey

Visions of the Western Railways

1. If you are keeping fifteen hundred out of say six thousand books which ones do you keep and why?

2. If you keep books you think you might not find again which isn't true of most books nevertheless why?

3. Let us suppose anyone would keep a book in black cloth spine lettered gilt *THE PURSUIT OF DEATH* / [floral motif] / *KURTZ*.

4. Various disbound Byron pamphlets for their nakedness. Also Churchill and Pope. Even Whitehead's *Honour, A Satire. Manners, A Satire.*

5. Books published when poetry was made wide-leaded. Romantics still wrote for such a spacious line. Check compositional changes after say 1820. The effect of the cramping of text in Victorian editions. After Anderson's Poets.

6. You do not keep Anderson's Poets although it includes many poets rarely again reprinted partly because it wants too much shelf-room and the leather on this set has rotted but even so you wouldn't disbind it or would you?

7. The poetry you keep is in any case what you remember and revise in your memory so what use books when the answer to textualism is as clear as that?

8. If for reference then with reference to what?

9. If you keep both Captain Thompson's and Margoliouth's Marvell what kind of love is that?

10. Various Chattertons. You might never read Bowles's Sonnets but isn't this pair even in the eighth edition a pretty thing?

11. What hasn't that to do with literary criticism? What kind of aesthete are you to think it?

12. [Richard Owen Cambridge's] *Scribleriad* for its engravings. Some poetry is worth whatever it inspired an engraver to.

13. Too many Miltons doesn't mean ditching a Bentley.

14. Sir Kenelm Digby's *Two Treatises: In the one of which, The Nature of Bodies; In the other, The Nature of Mans Soul, Is Looked Into: In Way of Discovery of the Immortality of Reasonable Souls* because it feels as if it must be poetry if not in name.

15. The Chaucer of probably 1561 lacking title but with spider doodles and dearest our initials G and A.

16. A couple of emblem books even as the binder's gilt says QUARLE'S and a tiny *Pia Desideria* although you'll never read Latin again. *Blake's Graphic Work and the Emblematic Tradition* because you tried writing emblems once.

17. The Garland facsimile Shelleys the masterpiece of language writing.

18. Some bibliographies including Foxon for all the disbound pamphlets you'll never own.

19. *Ulysses* five or six editions including for his witty name the Gabler. *Finnegans Wake* and its recensions. Umpteen Beckett and Wittgenstein. The *Cantos* in separate and collected editions. *Antheil and The Treatise on Harmony* effectively retitled in black ink: 'To certify that E Swainson having bought same refused 10 fr. reimbursement. — the authors increased esteem EPound 1926'.

20. Various contemporaries particularly my wife.

21. Pamphlets Bill Griffiths handmade. Books you see across a room were designed by Glenn Storhaug.

22. *The Dawn in Britain* in six volumes more readable wide-leaded.

23. Folios such as Sandys' Ovid and most elephant and elegant of all the 1718 Prior.

24. *The Landscape* for its typeface. *Christabel* with the pencil inscription *!'Folly, Folly. all is Folly'!*

25. Dodsley's Poems. Percy's Reliques. The more legible of Gay's Poems in quarto. Oxford English Texts preferably before they greyed in offset.

26. Friends and best enemies.

27. For the title on its spine alone and why not *VISIONS OF THE WESTERN RAILWAYS 1838*.

Situations

Sigurdur Gudmundsson

Structures, 1977
Mountain, 1980/82
Ljód, Hestur og Lestur, 1972
Camouflage, 1974

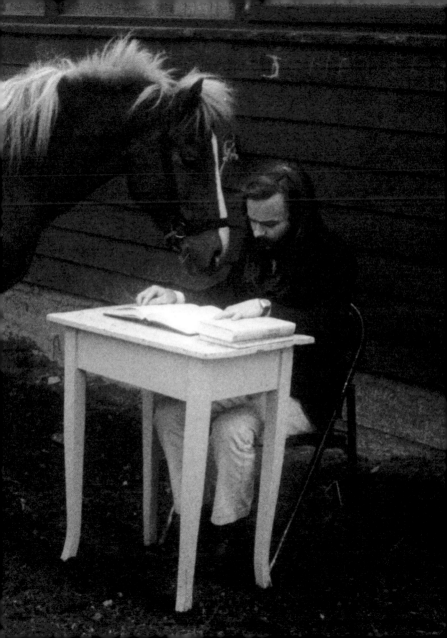

Field Guide

Hans Waanders
Jenny Brownrigg

The Field Guides of Hans Waanders

In Peter Carey's novel *Oscar and Lucinda*, Oscar is petrified of the sea. In order to make a necessary voyage over such a continuous mass, he carries a piece of celluloid onto which he has drawn a grid. A fellow passenger asks him how such a strange device will alleviate his horror: 'Oscar then explained his plan for viewing water through the celluloid. He could then view it one square at a time, thus containing it. What was terrifying in a vast expanse would become "quite manageable".'

The system of the grid will, in theory, restore to the observer a degree of control over the potentially limitless ocean. Placed between subject and object it creates a safe distance, reducing infinity to a human scale.

Similarly, it is the nature of the Field Guide, a book genre in which Hans Waanders chooses to make interventions, to contain immensity. Such books frame their subject matter (in Waanders case ornithology, lepidoptera and modern aviation) by utilising exhaustive systems of identification and classification. The subject is pinned down and presented for the viewer in a logical and comprehensive manner. An occurrence that is highly unlikely in reality becomes commonplace on the page: in *The Observer's Book of Birds*, the flights of bullfinch, chaffinch, house martin and wheat-ear are frozen in rigid formation. The birds have been reduced to a repeating pattern; all fly in the direction of the left margin, wings poised at identical angles. There will be no confusion on paper, as they remain fixed in our sights. We can return to the Field Guide at any time, in order to commit their features to memory. The only gaps that will appear are in the reader's knowledge. As one recognised category replaces another, the notion of the unknown is eliminated. The 'grid' that empiricism imposes allows the observer to control nature, within the limits of the book.

In Hans Waanders' book interventions, the static territory of the Field Guide becomes a freshly contested space. The artist employs the blue silhouette of the kingfisher, his chosen motif and the subject of his art for the past fifteen years. As an illustrative device the birds' silhouette aids simple recognition, with the subject reduced to a one-dimensional plane, a contained shape with a distinctive outline. The artist stamps a kingfisher on top of every bird which appears that is not of the species *Alcedo atthis*. If, on any page, there is a kingfisher, its image is left unmarked. The repeated stamps cancel out each bird, obliterating its features. Thwarting the process of identification, each bird is returned to the topographical unknown. Furthermore, the artist's interventions breach the confines of the book, with stamps appearing on covers – front, inside and back. The project spans volumes, countries, languages, time and singular species classification. The repeated mechanism becomes a ritual, reinstating the potential for a limitless and boundless space.

Through these actions Waanders shares territorial traits with the kingfisher, which establishes its territory with its call. He forges his own terrain within a space belonging to another; his process violates the sanctity of the autonomous printed book. The symbol of the kingfisher colonises pages in a methodical take-over. Frequently its image is overtly war-like; a dive-bombing kingfisher stamped onto a series of birds in flight. System fights system in this quiet invasion. These found books become the ideal place, habitat, nature and conditions for his chosen bird to establish itself in.

Hunting through the Field Guides to discover the untouched illustrations of the kingfisher mimics the real life preoccupation of the artist engaged in his own search for the next glimpse of this bird. When we discover it, the image of the kingfisher takes on a heavenly quality. Within the descriptive passages of Field Guides, observers refer to their sightings of the kingfisher in the wild with a choice of language that has celestial connotations – 'like a bright blue light', 'an electric blue flash'.

Within Waanders' books the kingfisher stamp marks time, until the bird itself emerges. Its appearance then is divine in nature. The repetition of its after-image, its shadow, is the required incantation in the artist's quests to become closer.

Waanders' interventions return mystery to the pages of the guides. Unlike Oscar's grid, his system seeks to expand rather than to reduce. However, like any system, it is human in construct. His marks mingle with the traces of previous book owners. A preserved newspaper cut-out is trapped in the pages of one book. Small, precise handwriting appears in another. A single foreign word systematically repeats under each bird where a sighting has been confirmed.

In previous interviews Waanders has said that for him, the kingfisher represents a metaphor of life – its possibilities, survival, flight and fall – and of mortality. After viewing his Field Guides the observer is left with an after-image, the weight of blue.

Jenny Brownrigg

BIRDS
OF LA PLATA

———

A King Penguin Book

2. Chingolo Song-sparrow
Chingolo

3. Scarlet Tyrant

Churrinche

6. Crested Cardinal

Cardenal

7. GLITTERING HUMMING-BIRD

Picaflor

12. RED OVEN-BIRD
Hornero

13. PAMPAS WOODPECKER
Carpintero

14. Firewood-Gatherer
Espinero

15. Spur-Winged Lapwing

Teru Teru

Previous pages: Field Guide
Hans Waanders, 2000

Birds of La Plata
W. H. Hudson, Penguin, 1952

Book Things

Shepherd Steiner
Rodney Graham

Book Things

What kind of a thing is a bookmark? Consider Rodney Graham's bookmark *Dr. No*, 1991. As a supplement to the infamous centipede scene, Graham's page-size bookmark fits seamlessly between pages 56 and 57 of the Pan Books edition of the Ian Fleming classic. Obviously it is no ordinary bookmark. Just as the deadly insect is poised to crawl off Bond's head at the bottom of page 56, and onto the pillow where he will kill it at the top of page 57, Graham's insert has the centipede crawl down and up the length of Bond's body again. We are confronted with just how expressive and even diabolical a medium the often forgotten bookmark can be. A moment of absolute dread is distilled and elongated. But there is something eclipsing the limited question of the bookmark that is far more unsettling here. In this instance it revolves around certain fears or desires that accompany one's entry into the book, and equally with obsessions found waiting there, which are carried back out into the world and linger long after the book is laid down. I refer to the complex of problems that intend upon any reader's entrance to, or leavetaking, from the ordinary book – of which the bookmark is only one of many portals.

Certain things about books are taken for granted. How one reads or enters the literary work is one of them. How these conditions of reading change over time is another. In large part Graham's practice is an attempt to think the 'nature' of what constitutes a literary work. And by 'nature', I refer not to a metaphysics that treats of the essence of the work, but rather to the conditions of possibility that lend the literary object the semblance of an essence in the first place. For instance, what differentiates the literary object and its space – dream-like and immanent – from the world at large or, what lends the text a material status in the world, a 'life' that allows it to circulate within a general economy?

It is in order to speak precisely to this set of concerns which '*make present* . . . (or) ensure the texts presence in the world, its "reception" and consumption in the form of a book' that Gèrard Genette singles out the notion of the paratext in *Paratexts: Thresholds of Interpretation*. For Genette, one's ability to read or enter a text hinges on a disparate set of conventions that perform a mediating role between the different infinities of the text and the reader. And though he freely admits that every context or frame serves as a sort of paratext, it may come as quite a shock that his interest devolves specifically upon the rather banal stock and trade of the bookmaker and publisher. The title, a frontispiece, the author's name, a publisher's colophon, the binding, format, or dimension, the fact of a bookmark, etc. perform an invaluable service. These sundry apparatus, which make of the raw text a literary object, prepare the ground for reading by naturalising the exchange relation upon which any entrance to a text depends. Genette writes:

> More than a boundary or a sealed border, the paratext is, rather, a *threshold*, or – a word Borges used apropos of a preface – a 'vestibule' that offers the world at large the possibility of either stepping inside or turning back. It is an 'undefined zone' between the inside and the outside, a zone without any hard and fast boundary on either the inward side (turned toward the text) or the outward side (turned toward the world's discourse about the text), an edge, or, as Phillipe Lejeune puts it, 'a fringe of the printed text which controls one's whole reading of the text.' Indeed, this fringe, always the conveyor of a commentary that is authorial or more or less legitimated by the author, constitutes a zone between text and off-text, a zone not only of transition but also of transaction.

Threshold figures are a commonplace in Graham's work. One finds the paratext guarding the literary work from an alien setting, framing an appropriation, reframing an extant work of literature, and introducing a new work, a pendant or an interpolation. One confronts the fetish character of the rare book or first edition, as a well as the devices and language of the pocket-book. The consummate bibliophile, all of Graham's literary objects hinge on an obsession with the occupational minutiae of the Republic of Letters. In some cases artistic intention is inseparable from the performance of an identity as a maker of books. Take for instance Graham's *Reading Machine for Lenz*, 1993, where the typesetting of the first 1434 words of C. R. Mueller's translation of Georg Büchner's novella are turned into a five-page text loop by virtue of 'two occurrences of the phrase *through the forest* in mutually compatible grammatical contexts.' Just as in Graham's earlier book, *Lenz* (1983), where questions of typesetting, the folding of folio sheets, the arrangement of a signature, and the interleafing of other signatures make up a 336 page, cloth-bound book with slipcase, the sorting out of paratexual matters is consubstantial with sculptural realisation.

What this obsession with the threshold figures of the paratext amounts to should be familiar enough to the adept. It is part and parcel of Graham's allegorical vision. Always subordinate to the text because of its instrumental function, the promise that the paratext holds out is the continually repressed material of reading: a movement that narrates our continual entrance and exit from the literary work. That Graham's *Reading Machine for Lenz* pushes Büchner's unfinished book from its famed status as Romantic page-turner into something far more obsessive, far more circular in its logic, is all too *apropos*. In Graham's work what constitutes the ideality of the literary object is reframed. What enables the book to be present is reinvented. It becomes another sort of thing altogether: perhaps a forerunner of cinema. In any case, given this dislocation of readerly expectations, it is worth remembering how very strange a thing a book actually is.

Shepherd Steiner

Reading Machine for Lenz

Rodney Graham, 1993 (courtesy of Lisson Gallery)

From an Auctioneer's Catalogue
Alan Halsey

[Anon.] *Facetus me Fecit, an Epistle from Cambridge*, 1735, 1st edn, folio, bound with *A Pom-Pom for Pomposity, An Answer to a Late Epistle from Cambridge*, 1736, 1st edn, some soiling, mod. calf. [£60–£80]

Barclay (John) *Argenis, with the translations by Ben Jonson & S. T. Coleridge*, 1842, 1st thus, 8vo, orig. cloth rubbed, partly unopened. [£10–£20]

[Beddoes, Thomas Lovell, pseud.] Theobald Vesselldoom *Chronic Steps, A Dramatic Pocket-book for 1833, containing Death's Jest-Book*, 1833, 1st edn, 1st issue with misprint to title, 8vo, cont. brds, worn, together with Thomas Lovell Beddoes *Studies in Anatomy, with other Scientific Treatises, including his Translations from the German*, 1852, 1st edn, 3 vols. 8vo, cont. calf, unopened. [£150–£200]

Behn (Aphra) *'We Taught the Whole Age to Love': Letters to Jack Hoyle, with her Intimate Journals*, 1974, 1st edn, 8vo, dw, together with Christopher Smart *Unpublished Prayers & Private Ejaculations*, 1978, 1st edn, 8vo, dw, with 24 others, scholarly interest and erotica. [£70–£90]

Blake (William) *Milton, a Poem in 12 books, from a recently discovered Manuscript*, ed. Geoffrey Keynes, 1935, 1st edn, 8vo, cloth in worn dw. [£30–£40]

Byron (G. G. N., Lord) *The Memoirs, Complete*, 1832, 1st edn, 2 vols. 4to, cont. calf, together with Lord Byron & Percy Bysshe Shelley *Journals of their Travels in America in 1825*, 1834, 2nd issue with usual cancellations, 8vo, orig. cloth darkened. [£70–£90]

[Clinket (Phoebe)] *Poems on Several Occasions, with An Epistle to J— G—, Esq.*, 1718, 1st edn, 8vo, cont. calf, brds detached. [£180-£200]

Collins (William) *Marginalia, being Notes Written in his Copy of the Holy Bible*, 1905, 1st edn, 8vo, orig. cloth, together with Sir Thomas Wyatt *The Correspondence with Anne Bulleyn*, 1965, 1st edn, 8vo, dw, with 10 others, scholarly interest & erotica. [£40–£50]

Dante Alighieri *The Divine Comedy*, tr. W. Blake, illus. throughout, 1834, 1st edn, folio, orig. brds, worn at extremities. [£150–£180]

Davenant (Sir William) *A Memoir of his Father, known as William Shakspere*, 1661, 1st edn, sm. 4to, orig. vellum soiled and buckled. [£150–£200]

Gay (John) *No Fools Like Wits, with An Answer to a Late Epistle from a Lady*, 1721, 2nd edn corrected, 8vo, disbound. [£20–£25]

Hayles (Ashley) *Los=Angeles=*, 1989, 1st edn, elephant folio, letterpress in red, blue & purple on handmade paper, 10/25 signed, inscr. to J. H. Prynne, cloth in slipcase, with 25 others, poetry & Blake interest. [£50-£60]

Hopkins (Manley) *Studies in the Work of Thomas Lovell Beddoes*, 1865, 1st edn, 8vo, orig. cloth, with 52 others, 19th C. poetry & literary interest. [£30–£40]

Jones (Sir William) *Britain Discovered, or the True History of Britanus of Tyre, with the Chief Druid's Discourse on Brahmanick Lore*, 1794, 1st edn, 4to, 28 engr. plates incl. 4 by W. Blake, cont. calf, joints weakened. [£80–£100]

Jonson (Ben) *Heroologia, or the Worthies of Scotland, An Epic, with A Discovery of the Loch of Lomond*, '1628' but 8vo reprint, bound with Ben Jonson *Epigrammes, the Second Booke, with his History of the Reign of Henry fift, Commonplace Book & Gleanings in Divinitie*, n.d., a late 17th C. piracy, some staining, cont. calf, brds detached. [£60–£80]

Jowett (B.) *A Commentary on the Fragments of Dichotomedes*, 1856, 1st edn, 8vo, orig. cloth, with 25 others, Greek philosophy & erotica. [£50-£60]

Kyd (Thomas) *Hamlet, a Tragedy*, 1589, 3rd issue with cancellations at B3 & C2 as usual, sm. 4to, disbound & heavily soiled, together with a small quantity of other plays, all reprints or pirated edns, incl. *The Isle of Dogs, Hot Anger soon Cold, The Late Murther of the Sonn upon the Mother*, &c., all disbound, some defective, sold w.a.f. [£250–£300]

Lees (Rev. Carlton) *Poems, with Judas Iscariot, a Tragedy, & Journals relating to the Use of Laudanum*, &c., 1885, 8vo, orig. cloth, unopened, sketch of family tree tipped in to f.f.e.p. showing Lees as illegitimate son of T. L. Beddoes [£10–£20]

Marvell (Andrew) *A Memoir of Mr. John Milton*, 1676, 2nd edn, sm. 4to, disbound, sl. soiled, together with Andrew Marvell *A Dissertation upon the Neoplatonick Philosophy, with other Papers Posthumously Gathered*, 1685, 4to, cont. calf rebacked. [£80–£100]

Pope (Alexander) *Brutus, an Epic Poem in Blank Verse, edited from his Posthumous Papers by the Rev. Wm. Warburton*, 1752, 1st edn, folio, later calf, with Montagu (Lady Mary Wortley) *An Account of her Intimacies with Mr. Pope, Written in Avignon, Now First Published*, 1820, 1st edn, 8vo, cont. calf, rubbed. [£120–£150]

Powell (Mary) *Advice to a Young Wife, written in the year 1644, printed from the original manuscript*, 1830, slim 8vo, orig. brds worn, with 15 others, Milton interest & erotica. [£50–£60]

Pseudo-Origen *De Maria Magdalena*, with the translation by Geoffrey Chaucer & a photo-facsimile of his manuscript, ed. F. J. Furnivall, 1875, 1st edn, large 8vo, orig. cloth rubbed at extremities, together with Radulphus Strode *Phantasma Radulphi*, ed. Furnivall, 1877, 1st edn, 8vo, with 3 others, similar. [£40–£50]

Ralegh (Sir Walter) *The Ocean to Cynthia, a Poem in XXII Boocks*, n.d. [Grolier 273: 'c. 1620'], 1st edn, folio, engraved t.p., a few minor repairs, a.e.g., mod. morocco with gilt Art deco device. [£200–£300]

Rawthey (Samuel) *Madrigalls & Ayres*, 1605, 4th edn, sm. 4to, some water staining, 19th C. calf sl. rubbed, ownership signature of Basil Bunting. [£80–£100]

Rowley (Thomas) *Works, additional to those Discovered by Mr. Chatterton*, 1794, 1st edn, 2 vols. 8vo, later morocco. [£70–£90]

Southey (Robert) *Robin Hood, a Poem in Ten Cantos*, 1834, 1st edn, 8vo, later green morocco with bow & arrow device, with Hartley Coleridge *Poems Vol. II*, 1838, 1st edn, 8vo, orig. brds, sw. shaken, and 35 others, poetry. [£70–£90]

[Spenser, Edmund, attrib.]*Epithalamion Thamesis*, 1585, 2nd edn with usual misprints & cancellations, sm. 4to, lacking title & final leaf, text complete, disbound & soiled. [£80-£100]

Swan (Thomas) *Poems, with several Papers relating to his Life & Family*, 1876 (Worcester Antiq. Soc. 2nd ser. Vol. VI),

1st edn, 4to, orig. brds, backstrip worn, some annotations & textual emendations in a later hand, ms. Poem '11,000 Leaves of Christ' & initials 'M.C-S' on fly. [£20–£30]

Taughe (Maureen) *A History of Irish Philosophy*, Galway edn, 1974, 3 vols, dws, together with *The Melancholy of Merleau-Ponty: A Symposium*, 1983, with 35 others, philosophy & sport. [£50–£60]

[Webster, John, attrib. to, with others] *Sesars Falle, a Tragedy*, 1608, 3rd edn, sm. 4to, disbound & heavily soiled, together with [?Webster & others] *The Too Harpes, a Comedy*, 1610, 2nd edn, sm. 4to, disbound & soiled. [£80–£100]

Weever (John) *Funerall Monuments, the Second Booke*, 1635, 1st edn, folio, with [Weever] *An Account of the Warres of the Poets* [n.d., prob. 1632] bound in, later calf, joints cracked, some staining. [£70–£80]

West (Colly) *The Poetical Works, with Notes Written in Lancaster Asylum*, ed. Richard Monk, 12 illus. by Richard Dadd, 1885, 1st edn, large paper issue, 2 vols 8vo, orig. cloth, extremities worn. [£40–£50]

Imaginary Books
Olaf Nicolai

Imaginary Books

Eye Candy for Magpies
Angela Carter (Henry Holt, London)

Long held back from publication by the trustees of Carter's Estate, *Eye Candy for Magpies* may well be Carter's greatest novel. It combines the faux realism of such late work as *Wise Children* with the unrepentant surrealism of *The Infernal Desire Machines of Doctor Hoffman*.

Set in contemporary London, the novel features Cynthia Gimcrack, a psychologist beset by fantastical visions that lead her to doubt the existence of the real world. As the narrative progresses, the intensity and duration of the visions increase until her every-day existence becomes a grey and terrible endurance. Cynthia finds herself inexorably drawn from the here-and-now, and husband Mark is ultimately unable to persuade her from this path.

The novel's paradoxical marriage of loss and fantasy creates a sense of catharsis unparalleled in modern literature. The knowledge that Carter had entered the final stages of terminal lung cancer when writing this novel adds a palpable sadness to the proceedings.

Jeff VanderMeer

Still Life
Henry James (Penguin, Harmondsworth)

In James' sequel to *The Portrait of a Lady*, Isabel Archer decides she deserves a better future. Divorcing her husband, feeling free, elated and more beautiful than ever, she leaves for New York – enough of Old Europe and the Italian countryside! – where, in due course, she falls in love again.

My alternative:

Still Life
A. S. Byatt (Vintage, New York)

A wondrous, meandering novel in which Byatt describes the life of Isabel Archer's niece, Liza, living in modern-day Sydney. Thirtysomething, single, independent and not in the least tortured, Liza uncovers Isabel's old diary and Byatt deftly narrates their parallel stories.

Lisa Corva

Telephone: Three Essays on Functionality and Extension
Edited with an introduction by Deborah Stein (Etc Books, London)

These essays – 'History & Sentimentality' by Clemence Harry, 'My Phone is my Home' by Jim Burke, and 'Cityscapes & Borderlines' by Chris Destri – consider our cultural experience of the telephone from emotional, psychological, historical and physical perspectives.

Telephone Line – No One is Answering
Jeffrey L. Ynne (Knopf Telecommunications, New York)

Telephone Line is a novel about emotional addiction, tracing Ynne's love-sick protagonist through a series of imagined scenarios in which he fails to connect with his desire. This unique 'book' is only available as a telephone conference. (Disconnected; re-issue imminent).

Jorn Ebner

The Book of Tarantula

(8 vols, Aleph Books, 13a Rue Savinien, Alfortville, France)

A book without words. Alchemically buried beneath Ariadne's Bridge in Calabrian lagoon. Appears once a year, on Night of Piety when demon spider dances across bridge. Translated from Farsi into Latin by Bishop Bellonius Minus Sormosedia of Selkirk.

I have been beneath the bridge, and have gazed
Into the face of the Black Madonna.
One howling, midwinter's night,
I searched for the book in the black waters of the lagoon.
I was about to leave, when I heard
Scratches octagonal upon the flags of the bridge.
I huddled down and tried to pray,
But no words came.
The demon was dancing tarantismo,
And a thousand spiders were dancing with her.
Then, in the flickering light of the emergent moon, I saw,
in the water
a dark, bony face.
Her eyes were sable and her clasped lips were almost smiling.
I felt a bite on the back of my neck.
The stars were blotted out, and the world was held in total blackness.
Everything was still.
'Leave the bridge!' I commanded.
'In the Name of Agur Iziarko, Maria di Montserrato
And all the Black Madonnas in the universe,
Return'st thou to the Hell from whence thou didst emerge!'
The spider's breath faded,
The dancing stopped and the stars returned.

I washed in the freezing water
And as the ripples settled, I saw,
in the moonlight,
my slowly flowing face reflected in the surface of the stream.
The next morning, as the boat moved over the water
And the island receded beneath the Sargasso,
The sun on the heaving, golden waves made the sea
A mess of broken mirrors.
As I scribe this tome of volumes, eight,
I am on the island
Dancing spider ballets around the turning leaves.

(October, 1106)

Suhayl Saadi

The University Of Pittenweem, Library of Scottish Culture

Carmina Gadelica, Matsuo Basho (ed.)
The Highlands & Islands, F. Fraser Darling & M. Merleau-Ponty
A Drunk Man Looks At The Thistle, Arthur Rimbaud
A Treatise Of Human Nature, H. D. Thoreau
Poems, chiefly in the Scottish Dialect, Dante Alighieri
Rob Roy, Fyodor Dostoyevsky
Kidnapped, Jack Kerouac
Sunset Song, Knut Hamsun
A Window In Thrums, Italo Calvino
The Dancers Inherit The Party, Samuel Taylor Coleridge

Thomas A. Clark

The Armchair Mountaineering Club Journal
Edited by Alexander & Susan Maris (The Armchair Mountaineering Club, Glasgow)

'We awoke to an imperfect summer dawn – hideously disfigured by our blinding hangovers. We tried every curative we could muster, beginning with the fullest of English Breakfasts and ending with a stiffly medicinal brandy ... We set off for the summits, clutching our heads and shielding our eyes form the cruel morning sunlight – believing that we were about to die ... but miraculously we managed to negotiate the knife-edged crest of Crib Goch, aided frequently by Spy's 'Noggin Bottle' and by our painful incapacity for vertigo; however before long even the Liquor became to rarefied to sustain us and our company parted upon the slopes of Yr Wyddfa: half heading homeward; half heading deeper into the mountains ... ' *(AMC Journal,* Vol. 2)

Vol. 1: 1986–87	Vol. 6: 1996
Vol. 2: 1988–89	Vol. 7: 1997
Vol. 3: 1990–91	Vol. 8: 1998
Vol. 4: 1992–93	Vol. 9: 1999
Vol. 5: 1994–95	Vol. 10: 2000

Also available:

The Armchair Mountaineering Club Guidebook
(1896 facsimile edition).

The AMC was refounded in 1986 and, in the footsteps of its predecessor, continues 'to promote the aesthetics of Armchair Mountaineering, and to encourage the fruitful deliberation of contemporary art, within a comfortable and congenial atmosphere.'

This re-publication of the original *AMC Guidebook* of 1896 re-establishes the high aspirations and fundamental principles of the Club, and perfectly encapsulates the conceptual nature of Armchair Mountaineering.

The AMC Expedition Cookbook

Elevating outdoor recipes which take full advantage of ingredients from the wild: campfire comestibles from 'Heather-Smoked Wild Brown Trout' to 'Risotto al Funghi'.

Alexander & Susan Maris

The Violence Taker
Alasdair Gray (Bloomsbury, London & New York)

An early 'Wild Bunch' novel, notable for its similarities to Kerouac. Gray self-published *The Violence Taker* at the age of 17, under the pseudonym Hugh MacThistle. The novel is notable for the early appearance of the protagonist from *Janine 1982*, who is beaten up in Chapter 3, 'Whereupon A Thrashing Is Delivered, and None Too Soon.'

Jeff VanderMeer

The Book of Ends
Raymond Queneau *The Book of Ends* (s. l.: Eschatology Press)

Queneau's last and lost book was made by manipulating the last pages of the last books of 99 writers, including this one.

Stephen Bury

STC
Alan Halsey

STC: A Short Title Catalogue of a Collection of Works, Now Believed Lost, by Samuel Taylor Coleridge

Address to Poverty, An
Address to the Clergy, An, concerning the Two Bills
Adventures of Fletcher Christian, The
Alexander's Feast
Annals and Philosophy of Superstition, The
Answer to the System of Nature, An
Apocalypse, The, A Metrical Translation, with an Essay on the Use & Interpretation of Scriptures

Barclay's 'Argenis' Translated into English Blank Verse
Before the Fall, a Musical Drama
Bibliotheca Specialis of the Books of Emblems & Symbols, of all Sects and Parties, Moral, Theological, or Political, including those in the Centenaries & Jubilee Volumes published by the Jesuit & other Religious Orders
Brook, The, a Poem dedicated to the Committee of Public Safety
Burnet's 'Theoria Telluris Sacra' in English Blank Verse

Carthon, an Opera
Character of Moses, The
Characteristics of Shakespear's Dramatic Works, with a Critical Review of each Play & a Critique of the Dramatic Works of Jonson, Massinger, & Beaumont & Fletcher
Christabel, with Essays on the 'Preternatural' & on Metre
Christianity the One True Philosophy
Comforts & Consolations from the exercise & right application of the Reason, the Imagination, and the Moral Feelings, addressed especially to those in Sickness, Adversity, or Distress of Mind, from speculative Gloom

Commentary on the Revelation, A, with Regard to the Progress of Natural Philosophy

Complete Works of Fulke Greville, The, with Notes

Complete Works of J. C. F. von Schiller, translated from the German

Crotchets

Defence of Aristotle & the Ancients, A

Defence of Christianity, A

Delirium, with The Soother of Absence & other Poems

Despotism and Ochlocracy

Destruction of Jerusalem under Titus, The, An Epic Poem

Dialogues on a Walking-Tour

Disquisitions respecting the Egyptian Theology & the Mysteries of Ancient Greece

Egomist, a Metaphysical Rhapsody

Eidoloclastes

Elementary Instruction of Children in Latin & Greek, The

Epistle to Mrs. Wollstonecraft, An

Escapes from Misery, with other Poems

Essay in Defence of Punning, An

Essay on Berkeley, An

Essay on Criticism, An

Essay on Sexual Psychology, An

Essay on Solitary Confinement, An, addressed to Sir Francis Burdett

Essay on the Adultery Bill, An

Essay on the Rev. W. L. Bowles

Essay on Tobit, An

Essays on Property as the Basis of Government
Excursion of Thor, The, A Poem in the Manner of Dante
Exotics Naturalized

Fable of the Four Wheels, The
Faust, Translated from the German of Goethe
First Navigator, The, from the German of Gessner
Five Lectures on Contemporary Poets
Five Treatises on the Logos, or Communicative & Communicable Intellect,
     in God and Man
Fragments of Heraclitus, The, Translated into English Verse
Future Inhabitation of the Moon, The, an Atheistic Romance

Grammar of the Greek Language, A
Grammatical Essays in respect to Gender & the Harmony of various
     Languages
Growth of Language, The
Growth of the Ludicrous, The, & its Influence on Poetry & Morals

Historie and Gests of Maxilian Cosmencephalus, The, or the Complete Book
     of the Two Worlds, Translated from the Original Esoteric into the
     Language of the Border Land
History of Logic, The, with a Compendium of Aristotelean Logic prefixed
History of Metaphysics in Germany, The
History of Phrases, The
History of Speculative Philosophy, The
History of the Levellers, The
Hymen of Athens, a Poem
Hymn to Dr. Darwin, in the Orphic Manner
Hymns to The Sun, The Moon, & The Elements

Imitations from the Modern Latin Poets

Jonas, a Monodrama

Kubla Khan, a Poem in Twelve Books

Lamentations of Jeremiah Sneak, The
Lecture on Metals, A
Lectures on the Principles Common to all the Fine Arts
Lectures on the Principles of Poetry
Letter to William Wordsworth concerning 'The Recluse', A
Letters from Germany
Letters on the Old and the New Testament, addressed to a Candidate for Holy Orders
Letters to William Godwin
Life & Writings of Jacob Behmen, The
Life & Writings of Giordano Bruno, The
Life of Dr. Beddoes, The
Life of Charles James Fox, The
Life of David, The, with other Sermons
Life of John Henderson, The
Life of Holtz, The, with Specimens of his Poems, translated or freely imitated in English Verse
Life of Lessing, The
Life of St. Theresa of Avila, The
Logosophia

Maniac, The, with Lack-wit & the Clock, & other Poems
Men & The Times, with his Newspaper Essays
Men and Women, a Novel

Methodus et Epochae, or Disquisition on God, Nature, and Man, containing the whole Scheme of the Dynamic Philosophy
Millennium, an History
Milton, a Monody, with other Poems

Naked Savage & the Gymnosophist, The
Nonsense Verses & Metrical Experiments, with Specimens derived from the German & Italian

Oberon, translated from the German of Wieland
Observations on the Proverb 'Extremes Meet'
Ode to Solitude, Nature & Liberty, with an Ode to Music
Odes: To A Looking Glass, St. Withold, To Southey, To a Moth, &c.
Of Calumny, Credulity & the Causes of Deceit & Error
On Abstract Ideas
On Dreams, Visions, Ghosts & Witchcraft
On Man, and the probable Destiny of the Human Race
On Marriage, with an Essay on the Present State of the French Nation
On the Art of Prolonging Life
On the Cultivation of Sunflowers
On the Nature & Uses of Character-Writing
On the Originality & Merits of Locke, Hobbes & Hume
On the Philosophy & Theory of Perception of Thomas Wedgwood, with remarks on his Mind & Character
On the Principles of Birdsong
Opus Maximum [Organum vere Organum]
Origin of Evil, The, an Epic Poem

Pantisocracy, or a practical Essay on the Abolition of Individual Property
Papers on Positive Theology

Paradise of Flowers' & Butterflies' Spirits, The

Petit Soulagement, Le, or Little Comforts, by a Valetudinarian

Philosophical Analysis of the Genius & Works of Dante, Spenser, Milton, Cervantes, & Calderon, A

Philosophical Examination of the British Constitution, A

Philosophical Letters to Josiah Wedgwood

Pleasures of Religion, The

Poems of a Methodist Parson: on Chemistry & Witchcraft

Poems of Mark Akenside, The

Poems of William Collins & Thomas Gray, The, with a Preliminary Dissertation

Poems of Richard Crashaw, The, with Notes &c

Poems on Infancy

Poems on the Naming of Places

Poetic Works of Milton, The, with Notes, &c

Progress of Liberty, The, a Poem

Proofs of the Antiquity of Welsh Bardism as a System of Quakerism

Propyleum, on the Power & Uses of Words

Reflections Moral and Political grounded on Information obtained during two years' Resident in Italy and the Mediterranean

Relics of my School-boy Muse, being fragments of poems composed before my fifteenth year

Revelations & Visions, with a series of Sapphic Poems

Revolutionary Minds: St. Thomas Aquinas, Duns Scotus, Martin Luther & Richard Baxter

Russia, a Poem, with the Deserts of Arabia, &c

Siberian Exiles, The, A Drama

Skeltoniads

Sonnets, or Effusions

Spinoza, A Poem, with The Reading Fly, Anselm & his Coachman in Hell, The Dutchman's Visit to the Learned Pig, &c.

Strictures on William Godwin & William Paley

Tragedy of the Earl of Essex, The, with The Northern Lights, a Poem

Translation of Euclid, A, in a series of Pindaric Odes

Travels of a Protestant & Lover of Antiquity in the Times of Queen Mary, with several Ballads

Treachery of Renneburg, The, A Tragedy

Treatise on the Corn Laws, A

Triumph of Loyalty, The, An Historic Drama in Five Acts

True History from Fairy Land, or the World Without and the World Within

Two Satires in the Manner of Donne

Two Tours

Upas Tree, The, & the Tartarean Forest, with other Poems & an Autobiographical Sketch

Vision of the Maid of Orleans, The, with The Tale of the Dark Ladie, the Third Part of Christabel & other Poems

Voyage to Malta, A

Wandering Jew, The, a Romance

Wanderings of Cain, The, in Twelve Cantos

Weather-Bound Travellers, The: or, Histories, Lays, Legends, Incidents, Anecdotes and Remarks contributed during a detention in one of the Hebrides

Alan Halsey

A Bank of Ideas
Cecilia Vicuña

The Bank of Ideas

—Through a common friend, I sent Salvador Allende a proposal to create a Bank of Ideas, to collect and carry out the best ideas in the country. Allende laughed and said: "Chile isn't ready."

—I began to compile an *Encyclopedia of Disgust*, a document of the abjection, violence and injustice in which we lived: no one contributed to it, everyone thought our era was the *Encyclopedia of Disgust*.

—I started a *Dictionary of Come-ons and Insults*, taking notes as I walked around Santiago with my friends.

—I made several 'Museums of Hair and Fingernails' in shoeboxes. All were destroyed.

The sum total of our thoughts creates the world.

(The Chile of that time made this thinking possible.)

> 'Extraordinary persons we are NOT,
> It is because of the thoughts of our Sun Father that
> we KNOW THESE THINGS,'
> > said Andrew Peynesta narrating the Zuni
> > creation myth.

'and when I got there'

Hermione Wiltshire

Holocaust Memorial
Juden Platz, Vienna
Rachel Whiteread

Two Poems

Edmond Jabès
translated by Rosmarie Waldrop

Letter from Sarah to Yukel

I am going to die, Yukel, it must be, in this book we do not have time to finish writing.

I am dying within myself for this unfinished book.

How many untouched pages before us!

Yet are they without wrinkles, as empty as we think?

It is as if a shadow lay on them, deep inside and on their calm surface, shadow of an unhappy hand so heavy, so cold it seems lifeless at the edge of the table.

How heavy this hand at one extreme of my body! How heavy this heart in the moist hollow of my hand!

The book could have been ours. I thought it would be. I hoped so. This was clearly madness. What life could appropriate the book all for itself? Death could, perhaps. Then all these still untried pages would yield to the accrued number of words that nobody could read within time.

A book for no one, at the end of love without frontiers.

Tomorrow is another moment of the book to be deciphered.

Letter from Yukel to Sarah

This book stripped of words, Sarah, nevertheless contains our story because it is a book written by death, and we have been dead from the moment we lost our name.

A thick blanket of snow covers our words. They are so distant, so forgotten by our brothers that they are perhaps no longer even words spoken by humans, but distorted echoes of our buried screams.

The absence of the book consecrates our absence. Like me, you are alive only where we no longer are, that is, where all mirrors lie shattered at the foot of a single one, behind which we stand, immobile.

The void we are examining is not that of the book we are quietly plunging into. It is the void of their book, Sarah, of which we are a transparent page, hostile against any resurgence of symbols, any belated flowering.

Out of the silence of centuries, discrete words will, one day, surface for us and then for those who have gradually learned to read us in the void. Our book is for tomorrow.

> *(Does the book, here, take the place of love? The book is an object of love. Love manifests itself in the book by hugging, stroking, biting sentences, words, letters and, outside the book, by an unveiled pasion for the words become writing, fertile lesions whose lips we spread open like a vulva to allow the sperm of death in.*
>
> *'Your parts, woman, are the white abyss of the book which once bled for an unheard-of word the flood of our words has since carried away,' he said.*
>
> *But hate and love are also in the book: hate and envy of God quickened by an undeciphered text, a text under the text, for which the latter exhausts and consumes itself.*
>
> *There is fire in the page to kindle and snuff its whiteness, eternal morning of the first, the only book.)*

From the terrace of my hotel I watch how countless birds – the waves – die with spread wings on the water.

And I said to myself, this must be the way books die, given that they begin with words taking wing toward the sky.

At times, one makes a powerful effort to rise into the air, but immediately falls back, cutting a hole in the sea.

Our graves are not those of words, nor those of fish or seabirds, graves eternally moving. They disdain and disturb the order of time.

'There is no end to the sea or the book,' you said. 'Words unwind the transparent thread of days in the continual back-and-forth of their life and death left to themselves.

'Though the pen grow weaker and weaker, the book nevertheless continues writing, in white letters, to the end.'

Making a book could mean exchanging the *void of writing* for *writing the void.*

> *(Nothing is alike any more. Remains what is to be remembered, that is, what is still standing between what was and what is no more: simulacrum of object, of language, of light.*
> *Writing is the dawning solitude of the letter.)*

Edmond Jabès
translated by Rosmarie Waldrop

Notes

Notes

Pages 58–59: these books were all purchased by the artist in a morning's browsing in a second-hand bookshop next to the old Cairn Gallery, Day's Mill, Nailsworth.

Pages 95–97: the stone bookshelf is in Kelso Abbey.

Pages 100–02: 'Twelve Who Ruled' (1990), in the private library of the German architect O. M. Ungers in Cologne. The identical plaster classical busts each represents one of the French Revolutionary Communite du Salut Publique. Photograph: Werner J. Hannappel

Pages 113–15: acknowledgement is due to the concept of the Video Box, where viewers can record their reactions to television programmes, as shown in Gus MacDonald's Channel 4 programme, *Right to Reply*.

Pages 117–21: this project was initiated in the spirit of Walter Benjamin's essay 'BookCollecting' and of the contracts that appear in *Venus in Furs* by Leopold von Sacher Masoch.

Pages 123–25: 'Reading Burns to the Scott Monument, Edinburgh, 1999' is one in a series of Landmark portraits activating historical sites and buildings – the landmarks themselves always remaining outside the picture frame. The photograph is by Alan Dimmick.

Pages 131–39: the majority of Gudmundsson's 'Situations' date from the 1970s and are collected in *Situations* published by Mál Og Menning in collaboration with BALTIC Centre for Contemporary Art.

Pages 183–89: 'and when I got there' (1999), was first presented in Spacex gallery (Exeter), as part of the Free Association Series, marking the centenary of Sigmund Freud's The Interpretation of Dreams. In 1523 the artist Giulio Romano, who had been employed by the Vatican to paint the great halls, drew sixteen stylised images of couples in positions of love-making, entitled *I Modi* (The Positions) and gave them to his assistant Marcantonio Raimondi to copy and publish. The images caused a furore, Raimondi found himself flung in gaol, and Romano beat a hasty retreat to Mantua. The photographs combine interior shots of the 'reserved' end of the Papal Libraries in Rome cut out in silhouette after the infamous drawings of Romano.

Index of Contributors

Acknowledgements

Thanks are due to the following copyright holders for permission to reproduce the works in this collection. While every effort has been made to trace and credit copyright holders, the Publishers will be glad to rectify any oversights in any future editions.

DAVID BELLINGHAM: 'Bookshelf for Kurt Sxhwitters', first published by WAX366 as a folding card, 1995. JENNY BROWNRIGG: 'The Field Guides of Hans Waanders', first published by Centre for Artist Books (University of Dundee), © 2001. GERRY CAMBRIDGE: 'Caravan Essay' first printed in *Scottish Book Collector*, Issue 6/8. NATHAN COLEY: 'Reading Robert Burns to the Scott Monument, Edinburgh, 1999', reproduced courtesy of City Art Centre, Edinburgh, © 2001. SIMON CUTTS: 'Spring Staircase' from *A Smell of Printing* (© Simon Cutts, Coracle, and Granary Books, 2000). DOUGLAS GORDON: 'A Relationship Between Books, 1994', reprinted courtesy of Bernard Starkmann. RODNEY GRAHAM: 'Reading Machine for Lenz', reproduced courtesy of Lisson Gallery, London, © 2001. SIGURDUR GUDMUNDSSON: selections from 'Situations' reproduced courtesy of Galarie van Gelder, Amsterdam. ALAN HALSEY: 'Visions of the Western Railways' first published by Gratton Street Irregulars, © 1998. EDMUND JABES: 'Letter from Sarah to Yukel' and 'Letter from Yukel to Sarah', from 'In Place of an Afterword', in *From the Book to the Book*, trans. Rosmarie Waldrop (© Wesleyan University Press, 1991, © Rosmarie Waldrop, 1991). JOHN LATHAM: 'Noit Intercourse', 1960, reproduced courtesy of Lisson Gallery, London, © 2001. TOM LEONARD: extract from the Introduction to *Radical Renfrew* (© Tom Leonard and Polygon, 1990). EDWIN MORGAN: 'The Burning of the Books' extract from 'From the Videobox', in *Collected Poems* (© Carcanet Press Ltd, 1990). CECILIA VICUNA: from *The Precarios* (© Wesleyan University Press, 1997). RACHEL WHITEREAD: *Holocaust Memorial*, photo by Werner Kaligofsky, reproduced courtesy of Anthony d'Offay Gallery, London, © 2001. HERMIONE WILTSHIRE: *'and when I got there'* reproduced courtesy of Spacex Gallery, Exeter.

pocketbooks

01   **GREEN WATERS**
ISBN 0 9527669 4 9; 96pp, colour illustrations, reprinting.

02   **ATOMS OF DELIGHT**
ISBN 0 7486 6275 8; paperback, 208pp, £7.99

03   **LOVE FOR LOVE**
ISBN 0 7486 6276 6; paperback, 200pp, £7.99

04   **WITHOUT DAY**
ISBN 0 7486 6277 4; paperback, 184pp, £7.99 (including VAT)

05   **WISH I WAS HERE**
ISBN 0 7486 6281 2; paperback, 208pp, £7.99 (including VAT)

06   **WILD LIFE**
ISBN 0 7486 6282 0; paperback, 208pp, £7.99 (including VAT)

07   **GRIP**
ISBN 0 7486 6238 9; paperback, 208pp, £7.99

08   **DISTANCE & PROXIMITY**
ISBN 0 7486 6288 X; paperback, 128pp, £7.99

09   **THE WAY TO COLD MOUNTAIN**
ISBN 0 7486 6289 8; paperback, 208pp, £7.99

10   **THE ORDER OF THINGS**
ISBN 0 7486 6290 1; paperback, 208pp, £7.99 (including VAT)

Autumn 2001

11   MACKEREL & CREAMOLA
      A collection of Ian Stephen's short stories with recipe-poems
      and children's drawings, *Mackerel &Creamola* is a rich portrayal
      of contemporary life in the Hebrides, drawing on the author's
      deep knowledge of sea lore. With a foreword by Gerry
      Cambridge, recipes by Donald Urquhart, and an audio CD.
      ISBN 0 7486 6302 9 paperback, 208pp, £7.99 (including VAT)

12   THE LIBRARIES OF THOUGHT & IMAGINATION
      An anthology of books and bookshelves edited by Alec Finlay,
      gathering an imaginative selection of contemporary writing
      and artist projects inspired by books, bibliophilia and libraries.
      ISBN 0 7486 6300 2 paperback, 208pp, £7.99

13   UNRAVELLING THE RIPPLE
      A portrait of a Hebridean tideline by Helen Douglas, this
      beautiful visual book unfolds as a single photographic image
      flowing through the textures and rhythms of sand, wrack
      and wave. With an essay by Rebecca Solnit.
      ISBN 0 7486 6303 7 paperback, 208pp, £7.99

Spring 2002

14   JUSTIFIED SINNERS
        An archaeology of Scottish winter culture (19.. .. ..).
        Edited by Ross Birrell and Alec Finlay.
        ISBN 0 7486 6308 8 paperback, 208pp, £7.99

15   FOOTBALL HAIKU
        An anthology of 'Football Haiku'. Edited by Alec Finlay, with
        photographs by Guy Moreton and an audio CD.
        ISBN 0 7486 6309 6 paperback, 208pp, £7.99 (including VAT)

16   LABANOTATION
        A celebration of the Archie Gemmill World Cup goal. Conceived
        by Alec Finlay, danced by Andy Howit, and photographed by
        Robin Gillanders. With an audio CD.
        ISBN 0 7486 6325 8 paperback, £7.99 (including VAT)

Available through all good bookshops.

Book trade orders to:
Scottish Book Source, 137 Dundee Street, Edinburgh EH11 1BG.

Copies are also available from:
Morning Star Publications, Canongate Venture (5), New Street,
Edinburgh EH8 8BH.

Website: www.pbks.co.uk